PIECES

Blessings & Love,
Trudy Harden

TRUDY HARDEN

PIECES

WHEN BROKEN BECOMES BEAUTIFUL

This book is lovingly and reverently dedicated to Pastors Rick Bard and Adam Shourds, as well as to their vision for the Foundry. These two men have inspired, encouraged, and supported me in my attempt to write this book. Had it not been for their sermon series, this book would not have a title. Without their challenge and calling to respond to God's purpose, this book would only be an unfulfilled dream of mine. Their vision for the Foundry, a former Boys and Girls Club and five acres of land in the poor part of our city, to become a faith-based community development center consisting of a Christian preschool and sports recreation center for the underprivileged in our town is in the process of becoming a blessing to the entire community. I agree with Rick and Adam and their vision to raise future leaders from the children in the most impoverished parts of our community. All children are created equal, and they should have equal opportunities to succeed in life, both spiritually and financially. I trust in God that this book will help all of us achieve that goal and even more for all mankind.

Contents

Preface

Dear reader,

THE BOOK YOU hold in your hands is my personal story, written from my heart and inspired by God. My memoir has some bad chapters, but the end of my story is good. I have been a journalist most of my adult life and felt God nudging me to publish some of my memories for His glory and honor, not mine. Writing this book has inspired me and strengthened my faith along the way. The longer I live here on this earth, the more defined life's lessons have become. I felt God telling me to share the wisdom and knowledge He has given to me over my sixty-seven years with others who might be going through similar situations.

Loss has shaken my life, and it has taken me a long time to pick up the pieces and put my life back together again. My losses have made me aware of how fragile life really is and the importance of enjoying every moment God gives me. It has taken me years to see His purpose for my life. He is using my suffering to make me more like Jesus. I've learned God is good all the time and He can be trusted. C. S. Lewis said, "Getting over a painful experience is much like crossing the monkey bars. You have to let go at some point in order to move forward." That pretty much describes what my story is about. It is about letting go and letting God. I went through a lot of grief for a long time before I made the decision to turn it over to God. God doesn't want us to always be stumbling around in the dark. Isaiah 50:10 (NIV) says, "Who among you fears the Lord and obeys the word of his servant? Let the one who has no light, trust in the name of the Lord and rely on their God." When I made the decision to turn it all over to God, my life miraculously changed for the better. I handed over to Him every tear I had cried, every word I wished I could have taken back, all my broken relationships, successes, and failures, along with the scars they had left on my life. I gave Him my past and allowed Him to control my future, and He made something beautiful of my life. Every season has brought me challenges that have helped me fine-tune my character. I have learned from my past experiences, but I don't live in the past anymore.

My prayer as I write these pages is that my words find you wherever you are in your journey. May they help you along your way to a closer relationship with our Lord and Savior, Jesus Christ, who can give you the same peace and joy He has given me.

1

Blessings of an Imperfect Life

TODAY IS TUESDAY—MY busy day, I call it, my favorite day of the week besides Sundays, the day I am busy working for the Lord. I seldom let anything interfere with my schedule. I'm usually up early enough to read my devotion, pray, and have coffee with my new husband, Tom, before heading out the door to my Pilates exercise class. I always feel better physically when I leave, sort of like the way I feel spiritually when I leave church on Sunday.

Then I'm off to a local nursing home to play the piano for the residents there. I pray on my way that someone will see God's love in me as we sing those old hymns. Many of the residents aren't able to sing or even speak, but I can hear them singing in their hearts as we sing "When We All Get to Heaven," "I'll Fly Away," and "What a Friend We Have in

Jesus." The piano was donated by a lady who peacefully died there in her sleep. Ms. Virginia was ninety-nine years old and played the piano just a short time before she died. She left her piano to the nursing home in her will. She outlived all her family and friends. Her church friends and those residents in the Bowling Green Nursing Home became her family, and she shared her love for God with them daily. Her favorite hymn was "Blessed Assurance." I look at her picture on the piano today and remember telling her I wanted to be just like her when I grow up. The plaque underneath her picture reads, "She loved everyone." What an awesome legacy.

I feel the presence of God in that place and know I'll leave in a few minutes feeling better than I did when I walked in. I smiled to myself as I heard one of the workers humming and singing with us as they went about their work taking care of the residents there. *They are working for the Lord too*, I thought, *and they need encouragement.* When I asked for requests, an elderly lady requested "Yield Not to Temptation." I take several old hymn books I've saved over the years, and I'm amazed at how I can almost always find the music to the songs they request. That's a God thing 'cause I'm a willing servant, an ordinary believer who has chosen Jesus wholeheartedly to guide and direct my life in the way He wants me to live. God rewards those who are obedient, and I am blessed more than I could have ever imagined.

I believe people in nursing homes are the most neglected people in the world. The administrator of the nursing home told me when I first started coming there several years ago how much he appreciated my faithfulness in coming every week. He made the statement, "These people were just like me and you before they came here." I have never forgotten that, and I always leave praising God and thanking Him that I can walk out of there on my own.

Then I'm off to my local church, where, when I enter the doors, I head straight for the prayer room. I call it my safe place. I kneel and pray for those prayer requests that were dropped into the offering plate on Sunday morning, as well as for my family, friends, and myself. My favorite scripture to recite before I pray is (I call it God's phone number) Jeremiah 33:3 (MSG), "Call to me and I will answer you. I will tell you marvelous and wondrous things that you could never figure out on your own."

Several years ago when my husband Bobby died while we were on vacation and I felt like I was a million miles away from home, someone from my church was in that same room praying for me. Now it was my turn to pray for others. I have witnessed so many powerful and miraculous things happen in my church since I joined the prayer team. I always feel better when I leave, knowing I serve a God who hears and answers prayer. It helps me stay tuned in to God all day long. I've become a prayer warrior, and I thank God daily for the lifeline called prayer. I thank God as I get down on my knees that I can get up on my feet, knowing I will walk out the door and drive my dependable car that is paid for to my wonderful home, which is mortgage-free. There was a time in my life when I didn't have a car or a roof over my head. I know what it is to suffer loss.

My journey through grief and loss has helped me understand what Jesus meant in Matthew 5:4 (KJV) when he says, "Blessed are those who mourn, for they shall be comforted." I think Jesus is saying true blessedness begins with sadness. I have faced many challenges that seemed unfair, but I never once questioned God. I thank God for my Christian heritage. My parents instilled in me at an early age how to rely on God, and I am grateful for their example. I see my challenges that seemed so unfair at one time as God's way of developing my faith and trust in Him. He has taken my brokenness and made something beautiful of my life.

If you are reading this book today and facing a situation that appears to be unfair and irreversible, do not lose heart or be afraid. Perhaps God is using your circumstances as a tool to grow and strengthen your faith like He did mine, equipping you for higher service. Don't give up on God. He'll never give up on you.

> Wait patiently for the Lord. Be brave and courageous.
> Yes, wait patiently on the Lord. (Psalm 27:14, NLT)

It's hard to walk in obedience to God and live a life that is pleasing to Him when you are carrying a heavy burden. My hardships forced me to rely on God completely, which in turn changed my life.

I graduated from high school in May 1965, started Spencerian Business College in June, and married my high school sweetheart in July the same year. I thought I would live happily ever after, but God had a different plan for my life.

I graduated from Spencerian College with honors and found a good job working as a secretary for a large Ford dealership in Louisville, Kentucky. I thought I had found my dream job, as shorthand and typing were my favorite subjects. Part of my job description was taking dictation from four different bosses and typing the dictations into letters. My husband also had a good job, and life was good for us until I got pregnant and lost my first child to a miscarriage. We decided to move back to our hometown, and my husband opted to open his own plumbing business to take full advantage of the plumber's license he had worked so hard to obtain. He made good money, and life was good. I got a job working for the board of education, and when I got pregnant a short time later, I was so excited. My husband was a deacon in our hometown church, where I taught Sunday school and played the piano. I'll never forget the joy I experienced when Stefanie was born. I hired an elderly lady to babysit, and after leaving Stefanie for a few weeks, I begged my husband to let me quit work as I couldn't stand the thought of leaving her with a stranger. My husband's plumbing business was doing well, and he agreed. I did typing out of my home to make extra money. Over the course of the next four years, even though I wasn't working, we were able to purchase a new home.

Over the next two years and not long after my second daughter, Alison, was born, the economy took a turn for the worse, and my husband's business went under. I went back to work when Stefanie started school and Alison, my youngest, was two years old. I hired a teenager to babysit this time instead of an older lady and got a job as a bank teller, but my meager salary could not support us. In an attempt to save my husband's business, my father took out a mortgage on his farm, which I finished paying off when my dad passed away in 1993. The effort to infuse additional capital into the business failed; we lost our home as well as our business. My husband became very depressed and started drinking heavily. Finally his brother, who lived in Nashville, Tennessee, intervened and suggested he seek employment and possibly move to Nashville. I saw God's love through my brother-in-law and sister-in-law, who helped both of us find jobs. We stayed with them until we could get an apartment and back on our feet. The girls were ages 5 and 9. My husband quit drinking several times, and each time I had hopes everything would be okay. I didn't believe in divorce, so I tried everything I knew humanly possible to save my marriage and help him stop abusing alcohol.

The girls and I went through a lot during the eight years we lived in Nashville. I remember trying to help him stop drinking. He went to AA, and I took the girls with me to Al-Anon. We found a church and made sure the kids were in Sunday school. We went to counseling together, but none of it worked. I got a part-time job as a leasing agent in the apartment complex where we lived and eventually worked my way up to management position. It wasn't until I talked to a minister who helped me understand that God created marriage to be beautiful that I realized it wasn't God's plan for my girls and me to endure the kind of suffering and pain we were going through. God didn't want us to live that way. I remember exactly the moment I made the decision to get out of that marriage. I finally accepted the fact that alcoholism had destroyed my marriage. A friend of mine invited me and my daughters to take a mini vacation with her and her daughter to Myrtle Beach. I remember sitting on the patio of that high-rise condo, looking out over the ocean, and praying intensely for God to give me the courage to file for divorce when I got back home. I prayed off and on all the way home for strength and courage to not back down. I had threatened to leave him several times, but I never followed through. Sometimes it takes a lot more courage to get out of a bad marriage than it does to stay. We returned home late Sunday night, and the following morning I called my attorney and started the divorce proceedings. It was one of the hardest things I'd ever done. It broke my heart when I had to break the marriage vow I had made to God.

I know what it is to suffer loss from a divorce after nineteen years of marriage. Our marriage wasn't all bad. I have a lot of good memories of my ex-husband as he had been a good father and provider until the nasty old disease called alcoholism took over our lives. Alcoholism is a disease, just like cancer and any other serious illness. I was not qualified to help my husband. I wasn't equipped to handle what I went through living with him. I look back now and realize God was protecting me and my girls when he made a way for us to leave. I was an enabler, being the codependent person that I am, as long as I stayed with him. Life gave me something that was out of my control. I knew I had to detach myself from the problem and let my husband figure it out on his own. I knew I had to protect my girls, and I was not doing them a favor by staying in that marriage. My husband was forced to take responsibility for his own actions. He was in and out of rehab several times before he turned it over to God, who made him the changed man he is today.

Out of respect for my ex-husband, my daughters, granddaughters, and their families, I choose not to go into any further details about this period in my life. We all have chapters of our life that are better left unread.

Now I look back on my life and am thankful for the two beautiful daughters that came out of that marriage. It's only by the grace of God I'm here today writing my story. I am so thankful the kids' dad is a changed man and is such a huge part of their lives. He is a wonderful father and grandfather and is living proof of what God can do with your life if you let Him. I thank God every day for His amazing grace.

I fell in love and married Jerry too soon after my divorce. I had no idea he suffered from post-traumatic stress disorder.

PTSD is a serious psychological condition, and he developed it after serving two tours in the Vietnam War. He was a good Christian man, and I knew he would be a good father to my girls. He died one year and four months after we married. I went through the worst period in my life. It was God who got me through. I was divorced at the age of thirty-nine, remarried at the age of forty, and widowed at the age of forty-one. This was a period in my life when God gave me what I call divine amnesia. I believe God protects us by allowing us to go into a state of shock when something traumatic happens. My life turned into a real nightmare. I spent so much time trying to block out all the bad that it took me years to recall all the good. I had two kids to raise with a small income and very little support from my ex-husband. My family, close friends, and church family helped me, for which I will forever be grateful. It was a period in my life when I learned to lean on the everlasting arms. I developed a real relationship with Jesus Christ. He became my best friend. My God and I walked hand in hand.

Two years later I married another wonderful Christian man named Bobby. I know God brought us together. He too had been divorced and fallen on hard times. I was working at a local bank. He was a former police officer and had recently gotten a job as a salesman for a local manufacturing company. He was responsible for a large geographical area and traveled during the week. I had a second job managing apartments for a roof over my head and was barely making ends meet.

He proposed to me one night when we were trying to juggle dating. It was really hard because I had a curfew for my daughters and I had to be home before them. He had a son in college and a daughter trying to make it on her own. I had a daughter in high school and one in college. Due to our financial situation, my oldest daughter, Stefanie, was forced to drop out a semester and work for a dentist. She went back to school during the fall semester after deciding to become a dental hygienist.

Today Stefanie is a successful dental hygienist living in Nashville, Tennessee, with her wonderful husband Lance and their six-year-old daughter Ava. My youngest daughter, Alison, was still at home and had fallen madly in love with a wonderful young man she met at the Dairy Queen where she worked after school. She married Mark her junior year in high school, and today she is a successful certified public accountant. She lives only five minutes from me here in Bowling Green, Kentucky. They were married fifteen years before they gave me my first granddaughter, Ann-Riley, who is eight years old. She used to tell her friends she got married right after her momma did.

Bobby and I were married in September, and Alison was married the following January, a few days before her seventeenth birthday. Bobby proposed to me by telling me I was cramped up in a small two-bedroom apartment, working two jobs, and since he had that big old two-story house that was empty during the week, we should just get married. Not very romantic, but I said, "Honey, if you've got the dining room, I got the table." I remember thinking of the perfect spot for it, along with my piano, which I had stored at my mom's house.

Thirty days before we were scheduled to fly to Las Vegas and get married, he had a heart attack. I remember praying to God to please let him live. I had just buried one husband, and I didn't think I could go through that again. God answered my prayer. The doctors were able to do angioplasty since it was only one artery that was blocked. As we had planned, we flew to Vegas on a long Labor Day weekend along with two other couples. We were married in Little Chapel of the West. I remember writing our vows on the plane and carrying Bobby's luggage on one arm and my luggage on the other because he couldn't lift over five pounds.

Almost eighteen years later, I found myself sitting on the edge of a bed in a motel room, staring at Bobby's suitcase, which I would have to carry once again. I looked at the huge tray of sandwiches sitting on the end table by the bed that the cardiac staff at Sentara Beach Hospital in Virginia Beach, Virginia, had sent with me and my stepdaughter, Robin, because Bobby had just died a few hours earlier. I had never felt so alone in all my life.

Robin was outside pacing and making phone calls to loved ones back home. I was having flashbacks from years ago when my husband Jerry died, and I had to call his mom and tell her on the phone. I can still remember hearing her screaming over the phone. I didn't think I could make that phone call again. I was thankful when Robin told me she had already called Bobby's mother. Robin also took over and called her husband, who made the necessary arrangements to get us home on the next available flight. Perhaps that is why God made it possible for Robin to be there with me. Bobby's son, Bob Jr., had been there all week. When Bobby showed signs of improvement and the doctor said he could go home the next day, Bob Jr. flew home to his job and family.

Bobby was supposed to go home with me today to our home in Kentucky, I thought. I felt numb and didn't think I could possibly move off the edge of the bed. I looked down on my right wrist and read the words on a bracelet I had bought in the gift shop earlier in the week when Bobby was in surgery. The nurse told me they had put in seven stints and during the surgery, there was a tear in one of the arteries. Dr. Griffin had called in a surgical team to be on standby. She told me later she had witnessed a God moment in that room when Dr. Griffin had spent forty minutes looking at pictures, trying to figure out what to do. He knew Bobby was not a candidate for open-heart surgery and probably couldn't survive it. She told me the doctor stopped and prayed when he didn't know what else to do. Suddenly there was a change and everything went like it was supposed to. I knew then he was in good hands. The inscription on my bracelet read, "Don't worry about anything; instead pray about everything. Tell God your need and thank Him for all He has done" (Philippians 4:6). On the other side was a fish symbol and the words that read, "Find Peace in Jesus." Little did I know that would be the bracelet I would be wearing to his funeral in a few days. The few words on that bracelet sustained me, healed me, and changed my life. I had them inscribed on the bench at the cemetery to remind me and hopefully others who might be visiting for years to come.

It was at that moment I found strength I never knew I had. Perhaps it was because I had so many of my church family and friends back home praying for me. Perhaps it was because Pastor Adam had called and prayed with me on the phone. My mind kept going back and forth from yesterday to tomorrow. It was telling me things like, *What if I'd done this for Bobby while he was still alive, what if the doctors messed up,* and *what do I do about funeral arrangements when I get home?* Sitting on the edge of the bed in that strange motel room and praying, I learned how to live in the moment. I got off the what-if bus and stepped into the moment. I started singing, "One day at a time sweet Jesus, Help me today to do what I have to do. Yesterday's gone sweet Jesus and tomorrow may never be mine. Help me to take one day at a time."

All of a sudden when I stopped singing, I was able to get up off that bed, check out of the room, and give the tray of sandwiches to a couple with several kids who were in the lobby checking in as I was checking out. They looked like they might be hungry and were most appreciative. I felt like I was at least doing something positive by giving something away. It wasn't until I got off the what-if bus and stepped into the moment that I was able to pray again.

Robin and I had waited at the hotel instead of choosing to wait long hours at the airport, which was a big mistake. We allowed ample time to get to the Norfolk airport, so we thought. We didn't allow for the awful hailstorm we would get caught in on the freeway. It was raining so hard we couldn't see two feet in front of us, and huge hail the size of golf balls was falling from the sky. Robin was driving, and I was begging her to pull over to the side of the road like everyone else. "We are the only idiots on the road," I remember telling her. Robin had said, "We can't stop. We must keep on going, or we'll miss our plane." So I held onto the dashboard and prayed with all my heart for God to get us to the airport while Robin prayed the Hail Mary, a Catholic prayer.

When we arrived safely at the airport, I looked upward to a beautiful clear blue sky just as the sun popped out and said, "Thank you, Lord." I knew then God was with me, and my faith kicked in as I remembered one of my favorite scriptures from Romans 8:28 (NLT), "And we know that God causes everything to work together for the good of those who love God and are called according to his purpose."

When Robin and I were seated on the plane, I opened my purse and found the small leather-bound book titled *Joy for a Woman's Soul*. My daughter Alison had given it to me for an early Mother's Day gift. She knew I loved to read while sitting on the beach in the sun. I opened the book to where

I had left off and read "The Joy of Trusting God's Plan" by Barbara Johnson.

> Look at the life you hold in your own two hands. Is it tattered and shabby? Think about it. Might it bring opportunities for growth and gladness? What is going to be important one hundred years from now that doesn't seem important now? What seems important now that will not be important a century from now?
>
> In moments that appear unredeemable, watch and wait. Recognize the precious things; refuse to trash anything! Ask God to help you see things from his perspective. Take one step after another. Before long, in spite of yourself, you may notice surprising signs of hope in your own backyard.
>
> Trial and triumph are what God uses to scribble all over the pages of our lives. They are signs that he is using us, loving us, shaping us to his image, enjoying our companionship, delivering us from evil, and writing eternity into our hearts. Be happy through everything because today is the only thing you can be sure of. Right here, right now, cherish the moment you hold in your hands.

I read the work of other authors who wrote about positive promises from God that refreshed my spirit. It was at that moment I realized I must trust God and let him help me through the tough days ahead.

My faith kicked in as I leaned back in my seat, looking out the window at the beautiful clouds, knowing Bobby was in heaven and God was with me. I smiled as I remembered seeing God's love through Bobby's favorite nurse, Willie. When the ambulance took us to the hospital that first night of our vacation, Willie was the one who told me I had two options. Number 1, I could worry, or number 2, I could pray. I remembered telling him, "I choose to pray."

Bobby was on a special diet while in the hospital and knew he wouldn't be eating any fried oysters on this vacation, so I promised to bring him a T-shirt from his favorite oyster bar called Ocean Eddie's. The morning Bobby died, I was late getting to the hospital because I had gone by the restaurant to pick up his T-shirt so he could wear it home the next day. Robin dropped me off at the hospital entrance since it was raining and went to park the car. I went straight to Bobby's room, holding the T-shirt up as I entered his room, telling him about walking in the rain to get the beautiful sky-blue shirt he was going to wear home the next day. I remember it had the name of the restaurant on the front, and the back of the shirt had the most beautiful sunset and ocean scene with the words "Last Call" written underneath it. We were scheduled to fly out at 5:30 a.m. the next morning and were in the process of getting his release papers signed. I remember sharing with Bobby how I saw God's love through the owner of the restaurant who did not charge me for the T-shirt and gave me free bottled water. I noticed Bobby looked a little pale, and when he said he didn't feel well, I called for the nurse. His doctor just happened to be on the floor and rushed in with four other nurses who rushed me out of the room as they did the code blue thing. Robin had just gotten there, and we were escorted across the hall to the family waiting room. A few minutes later, the doctor walked in with two chaplains, and I knew he was gone.

Willie, Bobby's favorite nurse, went back into the room with me to get Bobby's clothes. I remember starting to cry when I saw the T-shirt Bobby was supposed to wear home that day and Willie saying, "Would you like me to put that shirt on him to wear home?" I remember smiling through my tears, saying, "Yes, I would like that." I remember I did not feel alone anymore.

It was midnight when Robin and I stepped off the plane at the Nashville airport. My daughters Stefanie and Alison and stepson Bob Jr. were all waiting to hug us and cry with us on the way home. I was relieved when all four of them said they would spend the night with me. My daughters slept with me that night in mine and Bobby's big, king-size bed. We reminisced about how they slept with me twenty years ago when their stepdad, Jerry, had died. I remember asking them if this was a rerun just before we drifted off to sleep from exhaustion.

I carefully laid the *Joy* book I had been reading on the plane on my bedside table but left my bracelet on my arm. Those two things became my security blanket for the next year, knowing I could pick them up at any time as a reminder of God's amazing power to give me strength and encouragement. I was like broken pottery in need of being put back together piece by piece to become whole again. I knew from my past experience He could and would do it again. My job was to get out of His way and let Him do what He does best. My job was to trust and believe in Him wholeheartedly and surrender it all to Him. That was the hard part.

It's amazing how God puts the right people in your life at just the right time. God is nearest when our need is greatest. At this season of my life, I can look back and see how God did that for me. I kept a journal recording all the good and bad and humorous things the first year after Bobby died. May 9, 2008, Bobby and I left for vacation and headed for Virginia Beach with friends. I had no idea I'd be returning home without Bobby eight days later and planning his funeral. I saw God's love through my friends who were traveling with us. Elwood, Donna, Mary, and Dennis were there for me the first night when we called the ambulance to take Bobby to the hospital. They were there to sit and pray with me in the waiting room when he was in surgery. They were there to rejoice with me when the doctors said he was doing great and could go home by end of week. They stopped by the hospital on their way home to tell Bobby good-bye. They had no idea that would be the last time they would see their good friend.

I saw God's love through the people who passed by and smiled at me as I was playing songs on the baby grand piano in the lobby of that beautiful hospital. I felt like God had placed that piano there just for me. I had no idea I would be having those songs played at Bobby's funeral just a few days later. I saw God's love through the staff at the hospital and the doctors and nurses and chaplain who prayed with us in the family waiting room after he died. I saw God's love and grace through my kids and sister-in-law, Judy, who had lost her husband a couple of years earlier. They went with me to the funeral home to make arrangements. Pastor Rick was available to preach the funeral. I saw God's love through him as he met with us the night before the funeral and asked us to share some stories with him. The funeral service was so comforting and special because Pastor Rick made it all about Bobby. He took his favorite saying, "Wherever you go, there you are," and helped us see the wisdom in it by saying it was kind of a proverb, that it was a reminder to live in the moment God has given us. None of us are promised tomorrow. All we have is today, and the Bible reminds us in many places to make the most of today.

2

Running with Endurance

I was reading the book of Hebrews today and reflecting back to 1978. I was thirty-five years old and ran my first mini marathon sponsored by the Green County Fair Board. I completed the seven-mile race in sixty-three minutes and fifty-seven seconds. I have the certificate to prove it. I didn't just wake up one morning and suddenly decide to run seven miles. It took lots of training. I was working at the bank and my friend Claire, who also worked there, asked me to go to the track with her on our lunch hour. We started out walking and worked our way up to jogging. We set a goal to run one and one-half miles in fifteen minutes. It wasn't long until we reached that goal and set another goal to run five miles. She was a much better runner than me as she was tall and skinny. I was short and stocky and definitely not built to be a runner.

The only time I could outrun her was when we were running in the neighborhood and the dogs ran after us. I was scared of dogs and took off like a streak of lighting as fast as my short legs would carry me. She would stop, point her finger at them, and dare them to get out of their yard and run after us. Looking back through my scrapbook, I laughed and shed a tear for my dear friend Claire, who died at an early age from cancer. I had cut and pasted a cartoon into the scrapbook that showed a picture of two angels talking in heaven. One said to the other, "Of course I look healthy. I died jogging." I had written our names across the top. We ran on our lunch hours and after work. At last we felt comfortable enough to sign up for our first five-mile race in the Taylor County Fair. There were forty-four runners, and I think I finished fifth from the last. I also ran in the Adair County Fair, where I got a trophy, mainly because I was the only one signed up in my age bracket. I didn't care. I was proud of it. We ran two other seven-mile races together before I moved to Nashville, Tennessee, attempting to save my marriage, which eventually ended in divorce. I think running helping me get through a very difficult time in my life. I was building endurance. It became my escape. I wrote in my journal, "I'm a lifer. I run on more days than not, and I see nothing that will stop me from running on most of the days I have remaining. I run for the same reason I eat and sleep—because I feel better when I do it than when I don't, because regular exercise, like regular food and rest, is a physical and psychic need."

Scripture compares the Christian life to a race. Endurance is essential in order for us to succeed in life. I was taking care of my body at the time but not my soul. If I ever needed spiritual stamina, it was then in my marriage. My husband and I were attending church regularly, and I was the choir director, but we were hurting and in desperate need of God's healing grace. I love to tell the story of how I was asked to play the organ for a month to fill in at the church where we attended. I told them I could play the piano but not the organ. They insisted till I finally said yes, thinking that after hearing me the first Sunday, they wouldn't ask me again. After the first service, everyone talked about how wonderful it sounded. I played and prayed for God to help me for over a month until the regular organist was able to recovery from surgery. I told everyone it must have been God who played the foot pedals because it wasn't me. Seeing the way God played those foot pedals for me opened my eyes to the power that is available to us all if we trust in Him.

I wish my husband and I had had that kind of faith as we battled the problems that led to our divorce. We didn't have God at the center of our marriage. I just wanted out. James 1:2–3 tells us to welcome difficulties because the testing of our faith produces endurance. He is talking about the inner strength that allows us to face all difficulty without quitting. My training for life has come through trials. Every time I faced difficult challenges, God built me up more and more through the power of the Holy Spirit. I was in training when

I went through divorce, and it continued with the loss of two husbands so I could endure through the next chapter of my life. I sought godly counsel, but I didn't spend enough time alone with the Lord. My attorney advised me to file for divorce, and my friends encouraged me to leave my husband, the father of my children. You cannot always depend exclusively on others to tell you what to do. I have learned over the years how to surrender to God the things I have no control over. I learned to look to Jesus through Hebrews 12:1–2 (NLT), which urges us to "run with endurance the race that is set before us, looking unto Jesus, the author and finisher of our faith." In those days I felt like Forrest Gump. I found myself running for no reason at all.

I prayed and prayed for God to change my circumstances, but instead He changed me over the years. I would rush into the day feeling I did not have time to pray. My burdens became heavier and heavier, and I wondered why God allowed this to happen to me. One day when I asked God why He didn't help me, I heard him say, "You didn't ask." When I allowed God to shape my life and put the broken pieces back together again, I discovered new depths of meaning and purpose. I woke up this morning and paused before entering the day. I had so much to accomplish that I knew I must take the time to pray. Today I rely on God's promise in Isaiah 58:11 (NIV), "The Lord will guide you always, he will satisfy your needs in a sun-scorched land…You will be like a spring whose waters never fail."

My parents were great role models. They ran the race of life with endurance and instilled in me at an early age the importance of putting God first in my life. I was the third daughter born October 4, 1947, to Marion Presley and Eula Pauline (Jones) Chelf, who took me home from the hospital to a farmhouse in rural Adair County. We lived in a small town called Knifley, Kentucky. My parents married while my dad was home on leave from the United States Army. Thirteen months later on July 13, 1944, their first daughter was born while my dad was in Germany serving his country during WWII. When the war was finally over in 1945, my dad came home to see his daughter for the first time. He was only with her nine days when she suddenly became ill and died. Little Marion was only thirteen months old. I can only imagine the joy they must have felt when my dad returned home and the grief they must have gone through as they made funeral arrangements for their precious baby girl. My mom told me Little Marion, as we always called her, was just beginning to get to know her father when God took her to heaven. Thirteen months later my older sister, Barbara was born. Thirteen months later, I was born. Six years later my baby sister, Maurita, was born. We tell her she must have been an accident as she didn't fit anywhere in the thirteen-month pattern. I'm really glad she came along as she continues to be a blessing in my life, as well as my older sister, Barbara. I didn't get the connection with all the thirteens until I started writing a church testimony as to why 1 Corinthians 13:13 (NIV) had been my favorite scripture over the years. My parents taught me that the secret of running with endurance was love. My favorite scripture reads, "And now these three remain, faith, hope, and love, but the greatest of these is love."

I thank God every day for my Christian heritage. My dad was an elementary school teacher, basketball coach, and manager of a small farm. He loved God, his country, and his family. He also loved the outdoors and any kind of sport, especially bowling in his retirement years. He excelled at all he did and always encouraged me to be the best I could be. He learned from his parents to put God first, and he passed it on to me. My dad was my hero, and I wanted to grow up and marry someone just like him. My mom was equally precious to me. She was a stay-at-home mom who worked hard on the farm and supported my dad. They were a team, and they worked well together. I remember being angry at God for taking her away so suddenly with a brain aneurysm at the age of seventy-one. But when I watched my dad die of cancer two years later, I was praising God that she didn't have to suffer the way my dad did.

I don't have any bad memories of my childhood. We led a very simple life. My sisters and I worked alongside my parents on the farm, spending our summers helping with the tobacco crop. We always went to church when the doors were open. I was raised in an era where on Sunday, you invited the preacher to your house for dinner. Whenever there was a revival, the visiting preacher might spend the whole week at our house. We children were advised that we must be on our best behavior or else. We knew what "or else" meant, so we behaved. My dad made sure my sisters and I attended White Mills Christian Camp every year. My dad also helped pay for those who couldn't afford to attend. I think it was at that camp I fell in love for the first time (even though it was puppy love and only lasted a week). I don't ever remember missing a vacation Bible school or a youth rally. I played the piano at church for revivals, weddings, and funerals. I played a lot of sad music and a lot of happy music in my lifetime.

My dad was my first and seventh grade school teacher. Sometimes he was my Sunday school teacher. He was an elder in the church and took his responsibilities seriously. He taught me to always put God first and give not only of my monies but my time and talent. When my sisters and I got old enough to take piano lessons, he told us whichever one of us followed through and played the piano in church first would get the piano when we left home. I have that piano in my living room today. It is very special to me as my dad made payments on that piano. That's the only time I ever knew him to make payments on anything other than the mortgage on his farm. The next most precious books to me, besides my Bible, are those old hymn books from my daddy's church. I read my Bible, and God speaks to me. I play my piano, and I speak to God. I remember my late husband Bobby wanting to buy me a baby grand piano. I told him how much I appreciated the thought, but no other piano could take the place of the one my father bought me. As a kid, I sang and played "God Is Love" a lot.

When I asked my dad one day when I was a small child how much God loved me, he answered something like this: "Well, you know how much I love you?" I remember answering him by opening my arms as wide as I could and saying, "This much." He answered me by saying, "Magnify that love a trillion times over, and that's how much God loves you." I also remember my daddy walking me down the aisle saying, "You know it's not too late to back out, don't you?" Even though that marriage ended in divorce almost twenty years later, I'm glad I didn't. From that marriage, God gave me two beautiful daughters, who have given me two beautiful granddaughters. Today I have a very good relationship with my kids' father, who by the grace of God, is a changed man. Today he is a loving father to his kids and an awesome grandfather to our granddaughters. It's amazing what forgiveness can do in one's life. We must learn to forgive others, as well as ourselves, in order to move forward. We must learn to forgive the way God forgives us in order to live a blessed and happy life.

God gave my girls a new father figure through Bobby, who loved them like his own and filled the void until he passed away. Their real father now has God back in his life and is serving Him in his church today. God forgave him and gave him a second chance. I forgave him, and God gave me another chance to find happiness. Forgiveness is a powerful thing. Jesus performed all kinds of miracles when He walked among men. He healed the sick, freed the oppressed, showed His power over nature, and even raised the dead. But the story in

Luke 5:21–26 tells about one of the greatest miracles of all—forgiveness. To me, experiencing God's forgiveness in my life and then being allowed to start over again after He lifted the weight of guilt and shame from my shoulders is the greatest miracle of all. God doesn't throw in jail all guilty people who have made mistakes and tell them they are just getting what they deserve. He offers forgiveness, reconciliation, new starts, and second chances to those who ask. He invites us to come to Him, just like He invited the paralyzed man to get up and walk. He invites us to walk in a new direction and sometimes run in a new direction. It wasn't my job to condemn, judge, or save my ex-husband. The only person I can control is myself. I have made, and continue to make, plenty of mistakes for which I need to ask forgiveness. I chose to forgive not because it was easy, but because I know I've been forgiven. I chose to love because I know I've been loved. I not only see what God did for my ex-husband and members of my family, I see what God did for me. If you need to forgive someone today, go ahead and do it. Don't wait, for your reward is great. And don't forget to forgive yourself.

Thanksgiving season is almost here as I finish this chapter and write about the many times in my life I have experienced God's faithfulness. I review all His blessings and pause to thank Him for keeping His promises in His word, which have helped me run my race with endurance. I'm praying that sharing my experiences will prompt you to believe Him in your present circumstances.

3

Experiencing Love and Grace

My husband Tom and I were passing through Marietta, Georgia, on a beautiful Sunday in September on our way to spend a week's vacation in Hilton Head, South Carolina. We were listening to a sermon about grace by Pastor Adam on the CD player. I looked out the window and saw the exit sign to Marietta and started having a flashback of the three weeks I spent there over twenty-five years ago. I had shared my story with only a few people because it was so unbelievable that I couldn't believe it myself. I found myself reflecting back on the terrible mess I was in at that time and started sharing with Tom. I knew he would believe me. That's one of the reasons I married him in the first place. He is such a good listener and tends to believe everything I say. On our first date, I remember giving him a short version of my life history and thinking, *He'll probably never call me again*, but he did, and I'm glad.

I met my ex-husband Jerry while managing Knollwood Apartments in Nashville, Tennessee. I was actually his boss. I was the manager for a 326-unit complex and executive manager for another 150 units in the same community. He worked in the maintenance department and was the best and most dependable employee I had. Having gone through all the management courses, I knew it was not a good idea to get involved with the employees outside of business. Our relationship started out as strictly professional until he started asking me to have dinner with him after work. Both of us had recently gone through divorce and were in need of a shoulder to cry on. He was so positive about life, and we had similar beliefs about Christianity. He made me laugh and forget all about the bad things that had been going on in my life. He was so good to my girls, and they loved the attention he gave them. I knew they were missing their dad, but I had no intentions of marrying Jerry or anyone else. I told him I thought everyone should be locked up for six months after a divorce as we need time to grieve and heal just like we would the death of a spouse. Jerry invited me to go to Maryville, Tennessee, to visit his parents and teenage daughter. They were such Christian-loving people that I fell in love with them before I did Jerry.

We were married April 1, 1987, in a little country church in Nashville, Tennessee, by the same pastor who officiated at

Jerry's funeral a short time later. Jerry was only forty-three years old. Life seemed to be good for us until Jerry lost his job at the apartment complex where we lived. One of us had to resign since we were married and could no longer work for the same company. All the employees and my property manager gave us their blessings. Jerry found part-time work for a short while. One day he came home and told me he had gotten a good job in Marietta, Georgia. I believed him and had no reason not to. I had no idea he was suffering from PTSD from the Vietnam War. Looking back, I see God's love through my friend and babysitter, whom I left the kids with while I drove to Marietta, Georgia, with Jerry and found a job working in telemarketing. I hated that job, but I went to work every morning at Maple Leaf Mortgage Company with a grateful attitude, thinking it was temporary and that I would find something better soon. I felt certain my eight years of experience in the apartment business would find me a good job. Jerry convinced me to purchase a new vehicle in my name, saying he would be able to make the payments with his new salary. It was the first time in my life I ever drove a new vehicle off the showroom floor and the first time I ever had a vehicle in my name only. I was feeling pretty proud that day as I drove a shiny new red Olds off the showroom floor, thinking this was just the beginning of a wonderful life. I had no idea what was ahead.

Jerry dropped me off for work every morning, supposedly went to his work at Lockheed Martin and picked me up every afternoon. We were staying in a motel and spent our evenings looking for a place to live. He picked me up from work one afternoon and informed me he had a surprise for me. We drove to a wonderful neighborhood, and he showed me a beautiful home, telling me he had made a down payment on it. I was so excited and couldn't wait to get back to Nashville that weekend to tell my girls. I had promised them life would get better for us. I had asked them to be brave and good and trust me when I left them on Monday morning with the babysitter.

I made arrangements to enroll the kids in school, and we even moved our bed to our supposedly new home in Marietta. We even slept there overnight to save on motel bills. I remember asking Jerry how he had time to get all this done and work too. He informed me his company let him off to find a place to live and that he licensed the car in Georgia on his lunch hour. I made the big mistake of allowing Jerry to handle all our finances. I had a small savings, but it wasn't long until it was depleted. Jerry kept telling me not to worry, to just let him handle everything. After two weeks I had seen no evidence of a paycheck, and I began to get suspicious that something wasn't right. When I confronted him about it, he informed me he was sick and had been to the infirmary at work that day. He told me the doctors there had found lumps in both arms and said it could be cancerous. He just knew it was from the Agent Orange he had come in contact with during the Vietnam War era. I was devastated. I don't think he ever had a job, and to this day, I have no idea what he did during the day while I was at work those three weeks.

I felt God's love and grace through my wonderful parents when I called home and explained my situation as best I could through my broken voice. I tried to hold back the tears that were streaming down my face. I had given up the best-paying job I ever had, a job which provided a roof over our heads, and followed my new husband to a strange town, taken a job I hated, and my life was falling apart around me. They encouraged me to move back home, stay with them until I could rent a small farmhouse, and get medical and professional help for Jerry. That's exactly what I did. Remembering the parable of the lost son in the Bible found in Luke 15:11–32, I could see the similarities. I was the prodigal daughter, and Jesus was showing his love and grace to me through my parents. The core of this message is that it is only by God's grace that we are saved. I remember asking God to save me and help me. I felt like I was in quicksand and kept sinking deeper and deeper every day. I kept a journal and wrote down scriptures and positive sayings to remind me that God was with me. "My eyes are ever on the Lord, for only he will release my feet from the snare" from Psalm 25:15 (NIV) is one of them.

I saw God's love and grace through my brother-in-law, Van, who borrowed his brother's cattle truck, drove to Georgia, and picked up my bed. Then he stopped in Nashville, Tennessee, and picked up the rest of my furniture, which was in storage, and moved me back to my hometown. I made an appointment for Jerry with a surgeon who recommended a biopsy. He also suggested we go to the VA (Veterans Affairs) because we had no insurance, as neither of us had a job, so, that's what we did.

It was summertime, and the kids were out of school, so I was thankful for that. I remember noticing how beautiful the trees were driving through the country on my way back home. I called Jerry's brother asking him what he thought I should do. He wasn't much help, but he did tell me Jerry had never been the same since he came home from his second tour in Vietnam. He suggested I take him to the VA Hospital. I knew then his problem was much bigger than anything I could handle.

The first thing I did was find a job. I saw God's grace through my former boss, who I just happened to run into in the parking lot on my way to answer an ad for another job I had found in the newspaper. He was the president of the bank I had worked for before. When I explained to him I had moved back to the area and was looking for a job, he told he didn't have anything at the time but to stop by and fill out an application. I did, and I was hired the following week as a roving teller to fill in vacancies for vacation, etc., for all his branches. I felt like he created that job just for me, and it turned into a permanent position a short time later.

I remember coming home from work one day, praying, when a state trooper pulled me over because I had failed to come to a complete stop at a stop sign. I sat there with my hands tightly on the steering wheel, asking God to help me. I didn't know why he had stopped me. All I could think about was not having the extra money to pay a fine should he give me a ticket. When the officer came up to my window and asked to see my driver's license and registration, I broke down in tears and began to unload on him, telling him my sad story. I sat there crying, praying and feeling certain he was going to give me a ticket. Thankfully, I saw God's love and grace through that state trooper that day when he handed me back my papers, smiled at me, and said, "Lady, anyone who has a Tennessee driver's license, Georgia tags on her car, and resides in Kentucky must have one hell of a story to tell, and I don't have time to hear it. I'm just giving you a warning. Drive on, be careful, and don't let it happen again." My tears suddenly turned to laughter as I drove the rest of the way home thanking God for saving me. Laughter is often the best medicine. I got my daily dose that day, thinking that scenario tells a lot about my circumstances at that time. *Not even the best fiction writers could think that one up*, I thought to myself. *I'll have to put that in my book someday.* I've forgotten a lot of things about my past, but I'll never forget the kindness and love I saw on the state trooper's face that day. I'll never forget the feeling of relief and joy I felt when I pulled up to that old farmhouse. Jerry had prepared supper for us, and we laughed again when I shared my story with him. I felt like I had gotten a break. I knew God was with me, and it helped me maintain a positive attitude to deal with the tragedy that was ahead of me.

Jerry was seeing a psychologist at the VA hospital in Lexington, Kentucky, on a weekly basis. He had been diagnosed as having PTSD (post-traumatic stress disorder). Dr. Eng told me he thought Jerry was making great progress. I met with Dr. Eng, hoping to get some answers as to how I could help Jerry. When I shared with him how Jerry had lied to me about having a job in Georgia, Dr. Eng said he didn't lie to me like a normal person would lie. The doctor told me he actually believed the things he was telling me would come true. I shared with him other stories Jerry had shared with me, like the time he crawled under the bed during a thunderstorm because he thought he was back in Vietnam. Jerry told me the worst memories were of the little children that he saw killed during the war. Dr. Eng told me we have no idea what they went through over there, and one of the reasons vets won't open up and talk about it is because they think we won't believe them. I started reading some of Jerry's books about the Vietnam War and tried to educate myself. He had been reading a book called *Winners and Losers*. I later found a ten-page letter he had written to the author telling him a little bit of his story and thanking him for exposing the political side of the war. I also was having doubts about moving back to rural Kentucky, but I felt better when I read the last part of his letter to Mr. Emerson. Jerry wrote,

It's a gorgeous day here in south central Kentucky. I just pray that I'm still alive to see many more. I fear nothing that is known, it is the unknown that I fear most. I want to close on a positive note. I spoke earlier of my wife, Trudy! She's my crutch that I lean on. This little five foot-two, pretty woman has an outgoing personality, is a positive thinker and has been rock solid behind me through these last ordeals. I take a narcotic (Xanax) three times daily, and as with all drugs, sometimes I seem out of focus or insecure. Trudy can put her arms around me or just merely touch me, and it's more comforting than any drug I've ever experienced. I truly love her!

December 1987 was a bitter cold month. I came home from work one day and found a suicide letter from Jerry on the front seat of my car. I rode to work with my sister on the days Jerry needed to drive to Lexington to the VA for his appointment with Dr. Eng. The finance company had repossessed his truck, and we were behind on the car payments. This was one of those days that started out good but turned into a nightmare when I got home from work. His letter to me was the sweetest, kindest, and most loving letter I ever read. I pulled it out of my scrapbook today and reread the three pages again. It was all about me and how I would be better off without him. It was all about how much he loved me. He felt he had so many physical and emotional problems he would only be a burden to me and my family. He asked for my forgiveness and told me he had already asked God Almighty to bless me and my family, who had been so good to him, and to have mercy on his soul. He asked me not to be mad at his parents and thanked me for making their life happier. I called the rescue squad, who combed the area behind our house looking for him. My parents helped me search for him in the wooded area across the road. None of us found him.

I saw God's love and grace through my sister Maurita when I spent the night on her couch. Early the next morning, Maurita and I looked out her window and saw him walking through her yard. He had garbage bags on his arms and feet to protect him from the cold. He smelled like smoke, so we knew he had built a fire. He seemed disoriented and traumatized. The mix of ice and snow made the country road we lived on very treacherous, but I didn't know what to do except take him back to the VA. I saw God's love and grace through my sister Barbara, who rode with me. It took us over three hours to get to the VA. I remember Jerry making me stop often to let him get out and clear the ice off the headlights. He was admitted to the psychiatric ward and stayed until March of 1988. I saw God's love and grace during that time when I received a letter from my landlord. The Nortoffs waived my rent until Jerry could get back on his feet, telling me they would rather I stay there and maintain the property during the winter months than leave it vacant.

My daughter Alison and I spent the nights with my parents since it was so cold and I couldn't afford to pay the high electric bills. I wouldn't take anything for the time I spent with my parents while Jerry was in the psychiatric ward at the VA hospital. Alison was a freshman in high school and road the school bus to my mother's house in the afternoons. My older daughter, Stefanie, had been approved for a grant and was a freshman at Western Kentucky University. Mama would have supper on the table when I got home from work. Her faith in God and positive support assured me everything would be okay. She not only fed my body, she fed my soul with her godly example. If there was ever an angel who walked on earth, it was my mother (Pauline Jones Chelf). I made visits on the weekend to see Jerry and met with Dr. Erling Eng, who assured me he was making progress with Jerry. When the weather got warmer and Jerry came home from the hospital, we were able to move back into the farmhouse. Jerry spent a lot of his time painting and keeping up the old farmhouse. He began searching for work and started cutting back on his Xanax. He really thought he was going to get better. Jerry suffered a heat stroke while mowing the yard one hot July day, and I realized he would probably never be able to hold down a job. Even though I only made $900 a month as a bank teller and my ex-husband was behind on child support, I was able to keep the bills paid.

Jerry left home on August 24, 1988, telling me he was going to the store to put air in a low tire on our Ford hatchback. The bank had ultimately repossessed the shiny new Olds that I had been so proud of. Jerry had purchased the hatchback from a used car dealership after borrowing the money from his sister to buy it. I never saw him again. All the days he was missing, I kept praying and thinking he was off on another one of his excursions, as he called them. After Jerry died, I found a letter that he had written to the book author Emerson about a book he had been reading. He stated that over the last thirteen years, there were periods in his life when he would seek total withdrawal from the world and his family. He would just take off into the woods to hunt the enemy and be by himself and try and figure everything out. I thought he would return in about three days. I went to work every day and saw God's love and grace through my coworkers, who supported me and helped me with my workload. I made phone calls at night to the police, his parents, the VA, the surrounding hospitals and places I thought he might have gone. On the fourth day, I took off from work (without pay) and went to the VA hospital in Lexington, Kentucky, begging them to help me. I had a notarized statement from Jerry giving me the authority to handle his personal affairs. I did not have an appointment, so I sat there all day. Around 5:00 p.m. the gentleman I was waiting to see came out and told me I would have to come back tomorrow. I lost my composure and told him if he didn't see me that day, I would follow him home and sit on his doorstep until he talked with me, as there was no way I could afford to lose another day's pay. When I started crying and telling him a little of my story, I saw God's love and grace through him when he stayed late and filled out my paperwork. Since they had no record of his disability claim, I left there in tears thinking I had lost a day's pay and gained nothing. As I was leaving, I looked up on the bulletin board there in the lobby of the VA and read this prayer of an unknown confederate soldier:

> I ASKED GOD FOR STRENGTH, THAT I MIGHT ACHIEVE
>
> I WAS MADE WEAK, THAT I MIGHT LEARN TO HUMBLY OBEY
>
> I ASKED FOR HEALTH, THAT I MIGHT DO GREATER THINGS
>
> I WAS GIVEN INFIRMITY, THAT I MIGHT DO BETTER THINGS
>
> I ASKED FOR RICHES, THAT I MIGHT BE HAPPY
>
> I WAS GIVEN POVERTY, THAT I MIGHT BE WISE
>
> I ASKED FOR POWER, THAT I MIGHT HAVE THE PRAISE OF MEN
>
> I WAS GIVEN WEAKNESS, THAT I MIGHT FEEL THE NEED OF GOD
>
> I ASKED FOR ALL THINGS, THAT I MIGHT ENJOY LIFE
>
> I WAS GIVEN LIFE, THAT I MIGHT ENJOY ALL THINGS
>
> I GOT NOTHING THAT I ASKED FOR, BUT EVERYTHING THAT I HAD HOPED FOR
>
> ALMOST DESPITE MYSELF MY UNSPOKEN PRAYERS WERE ANSWERED
>
> I AM AMONG ALL MEN RICHLY BLESSED.

I don't know why, but I took the time to write it down. I used it later in Jerry's funeral and kept it all these years as a reminder of how God answers our unspoken prayers. His unspoken prayers had already been answered, and I didn't know it. God knew better than me how to heal Jerry by taking him to heaven. I went back to work the next day exhausted. Like Jerry had said earlier, the fear of the unknown was what I now feared the most.

Three days later a police officer knocked on the backdoor of Community Bank and Trust in Columbia, Kentucky, where I worked, and asked to speak with me. He asked if I would come by the nearby state police headquarters when I got off work. When I arrived and saw my sister's car and a friend from church at the door, I knew Jerry was dead. The police officer asked me to have a seat and handed me Jerry's wallet, asking me to identify him. He had been found in the trunk of our Ford hatchback in the far end of a hospital parking lot in Russell Springs, Kentucky. He had been missing a total of seven days. I remember asking them why it took so long for them to find him. The police officer informed me the car had been parked there for several days before anyone reported it, and when they tried to run a search, the car was still registered to the car dealership where it was purchased. The officer said they found a napkin on the front seat with my name, address, and phone number. There were no signs of foul play, and there would be an autopsy to determine cause of death.

I don't remember much else about that day, except when I got home, I found another mentally disturbed veteran friend of Jerry's sitting in my driveway in his truck showing his respect. He didn't say a word, just sat there in his truck with his head bowed in silence. He nodded as I went into the house, and after a few minutes, he left. As I walked in the front door, I encountered another Vietnam veteran whom Jerry had brought home from the VA hospital and who was staying with a nearby friend. Jerry was trying to help him stay sober. Jerry had told me since we lived in a dry county and he couldn't buy alcohol, it would be good for him. I remember asking Jerry why the veteran was always washing his hands. Jerry told me he was a medic in Vietnam and was constantly trying to wash the blood off. My heart went out to him, but I set my foot down and told Jerry he had to take him back to the VA on his next visit as I could barely feed us and could not take on another mouth to feed. He was still there when Jerry died, and a friend from the church drove him back to the VA. Even though Jerry was mentally disturbed himself, he had a heart of gold and was always trying to help his fellow veterans.

My oldest daughter, Stefanie, was a freshman at Western Kentucky University, and her car broke down on her way home. A Methodist preacher just happened along on the Cumberland Parkway after dark and gave her a ride home. We had no cell phones in those days. I saw God's love through a Good Samaritan in the person of Pastor Mosley. He is a retired minister and member of the church I attend today. I introduced him to Stefanie at church one Sunday when she was visiting, but he didn't remember the incident when he had befriended her. I told him he might not remember it, but we would never forget it. God was with us that day when he brought her home safely. I remember searching my Bible for strength and guidance. I remember telling my kids everything was going to be okay. I was so scared, yet I felt a sense of relief knowing I knew what I had to deal with. I was so thankful I had my family and church family to lean on.

The next few days, I felt like Jerry on one of his excursions. I just wanted to withdraw and get away from it all. That's when God gave me divine amnesia, and the shock set in. With this being the worst days of my life, I remember God being with me through it all. The small community of Knifley, Kentucky, and the people of surrounding cities were there for me, showering me with food, money, love, and support. I remember having two funerals—one in Campbellsville, Kentucky, early Saturday morning and the graveside service in Maryville, Tennessee, where Jerry rests in a family cemetery, late that afternoon. I remember looking behind and seeing all the cars' lights in the funeral procession as we traveled the long way. I remember my sister Maurita driving and my sister Barbara riding shotgun. I remember sitting with my daughters in the backseat and coming home late that night. I remember praying just before we got home, asking God to give me a sign that I'd get through this. I looked out the window through the raindrops that were starting to come down and saw my neighbor, an elderly blind woman who lived by herself, feeling her way on a clothesline to the outhouse. I felt God telling me at that moment that I had two hands and was able to work and provide for my girls. He told me I had two eyes to see where I was going. He told me I had a lot more than Ms. Willie. I had indoor plumbing. Most importantly, He was telling me to trust Him. It was at that moment I leaned on Jesus and developed what I call a real relationship with God. I surrendered it all to Him. I went to visit Ms Willie later and shared my story with her. She was a wise black lady who lived to be one hundred years old. She was full of stories, and my daughters enjoyed listening to her as well. I wish I had written some of her words of wisdom down.

This is my story, I'm thinking as I continue to share it with you in the pages of this book. You might be wondering why I would want to write about the muddy seasons in my life. This is my way of honoring God and letting others know how awesome and powerful God is. It's also a great way for me to leave a legacy to my children and grandchildren. I want them to know the power of prayer. I want my grandchildren to one day read my story and say, "My grana was a prayer warrior. She made some poor choices in her lifetime, but she also made some right choices. She relied on God not only in the bad times but also the good times. She made the choice to rejoice every day, no matter her circumstances." I want them to say, "She was a victor, not a victim."

There is so much I could say about God's grace. I know that God has made me right with myself through His grace. I know that I live with God every day. I learned through my brokenness what it means to surrender it all to Him. I have been changed from the inside out. Surrender is powerful. Surrender is necessary if I am to become more like Jesus. I must get up every morning and give it all to God so that I can love others like Christ wants me to. Life happens, and just because everything is going my way today doesn't mean it will tomorrow. I know God will be there to help me through whatever comes my way. I know God's grace is truly amazing and that He is still working on me.

4

Rebuilding after Loss

I WENT TO Sunday school the morning after Jerry's funeral thinking I wanted to sow faith so I could reap some of the peace that Pastor Shelton had been talking about at Jerry's funeral. The Sunday school teacher began our class by reading a tribute to Jerry. He spoke of how sad we all were because we had lost a good friend and worker for the Lord. I realized I wasn't the only one grieving. Nolan spoke of Jerry's great talent being his love for people and how he had been so easy to get to know and love. We were reminded of how we were going to miss hearing him singing bass in our choir as he loved to bellow out as we sang his favorite song, "Just a Little Talk with Jesus." I realized then the impact Jerry had made on so many lives in the short time he had been a member of that small country church. He said Jerry would want us to use the talents the Lord had given us for the Lord's kingdom. With teary eyes, he reminded the class how I was going to need their love and support.

I remember one time after attending Sunday school class, going to the worship service, opening my wallet when the offering plate was passed, and finding only a one-dollar bill. I hesitantly placed it in the offering, knowing full well it was Alison's lunch money for the following day. We were in the car headed home when Alison said, "You're not going to believe this, but as I was leaving church, Nolan stuck a ten-dollar bill in my pocket." The following week, Pastor Shelton, the minister who had traveled from Hendersonville, Tennessee, to officiate Jerry's funeral, returned the check I had written for twenty-five dollars intended to offset some of his travel expenses. He had written across the face of the check in big letters "THANKS," and he had also included his own personal check in the amount of one hundred dollars plus a note that read, "Please accept this as a token of our love for you and Jerry." Reflecting on these two events of generosity, I realized that God does truly work in mysterious ways. I also finally came to grips with the truth expressed in the saying, "You can't outgive God!" I now had concrete examples of what Pastor Shelton had been talking about when he told me to trust in God, for he is the only true source of peace, a serenity that I desperately needed at that time.

Even though the days and weeks ahead were tough, I never felt alone or abandoned by God. It is difficult to hold on to faith when things go terribly wrong, but it does give peace to those who put their trust in God. The word *peace* comes from the Hebrew word *shalom*, meaning "wholeness and friendship with God." *Trust* is from the Hebrew word *betach* (meaning "standing firmly on something, like a rock"). God became my rock, my go-to person. I wrote in the "Good News Journal" I kept at that time, positive sayings like... When our need is greatest, God is nearest. "Our last supply becomes God's first concern," "I resolve to put my life back together and get to work on the rest of my life," "I will pull myself together," "I will make a way for me and my girls," "I will keep on praying and believing that God will be good to me," "I will have tomorrow what others can't 'cause I will do today what others won't" (this one stayed on my fridge till I moved from that old farmhouse a short time later), "The rest of my life will be the best of my life," "I can do all things through Christ, who gives me strength," "Faith is the mover of mountains," "She's single again," and "Good things come to those who hustle while they wait."

I prayed for God to fill me with the fruits of the spirit so that I might make the right decisions. I prayed like I had never prayed before. I had gotten past praying those three little words, "God, help me," to being more specific. I asked Him to help me do only the things that were good and decent.

I sit here tonight on this peaceful fall night looking back over the scrapbook I put together after Jerry's death. I am amazed at how much good came from that short marriage and my grief. Good things come from grieving. I have a book called *Good Grief*, which is one of my favorite. I love reading the funny stories. I've learned you can laugh and grieve at the same time. It is allowed.

I took a week's vacation from work after the funeral and spent a lot of time praying as I worked diligently in the bathroom finishing the remodeling job Jerry had started. I took my anger out on the walls as I used a hammer and crowbar to pry the old linoleum that was glued to the bottom half of the wall. Underneath that ugly old linoleum was a beautiful wood tongue and groove, which I later painted white. It was beautiful. Thinking back, that's like what I was doing for myself as I took steps to get better and become something beautiful. I was getting rid of the ugly. You don't go through grief and trauma and not learn from it or grow closer to God because sometimes you don't really get to know Christ until He is all you have.

My life was such a mess. There's no way I could have survived without God by my side. He gave me strength when I was exhausted. He gave me courage when I was afraid. He replaced my pain with peace and mercy. When I became doubtful and unsure, he gave me knowledge and wisdom to help me work through my problems. He placed Christian friends and family in my life to support and encourage me. I asked, and He provided. There were days when I didn't have a clue what would happen next, but by the Grace of God, I survived. I kept on asking as it says in Matthew 7:7–8 (NLT),

"Keep on asking and you will receive what you ask for. Keep on seeking and you will find. Keep on knocking, and the door will be opened to you. For everyone who asks, receives. Everyone who seeks, finds. And to everyone who knocks, the door will be opened." This taught me perseverance. I kept on asking in faith. Many times I didn't feel like praying, but I did anyway. Those were the times I relied on the Holy Spirit like it tells us in Romans 8:26a (NLT), "The Holy Spirit helps us in our distress." It must have been the Holy Spirit who prayed for me with groaning I could not express in words. Some of the words I used while working on that bathroom wall are not in the Bible, and some of them are not even in the English language. God knew in advance what I needed. Jeremiah 29:11 (NIV) tells me, "For I know the plans I have for you, declares the Lord, plans to prosper you and not harm you, plans to give you hope and a future." God had already made the plans for my life, and He didn't feel the need to check with me. All He asked was that I let go and let Him have control of my life. I saw God's love and protection through my nephew, Todd, who slept on my couch for a week after Jerry's funeral. I saw God's love through my brother-in-law, Van, who repaired the broken lock in the basement so I would not be afraid at night. I saw God's love through my sister Maurita, who left care packages on my front porch and made sure I always had a ride to work. I saw God's love through my daddy, who insisted he drive me to the salvage yard to pick up the measly three-hundred-dollar check that the salvage yard was willing to pay for the motor of the car Jerry's body was found in. He wanted to make sure I didn't make that trip alone. I continued to see God's love through my parents, who lived just up the road and were always checking on me to see if I needed anything. They always made sure I had a ride to church since I didn't have a car. It wasn't long after imposing upon my family for transportation that I saw God's love through the family who gave me an old yellow station wagon. That old yellow station wagon became an icon symbol to me of God's love. It kept running and running, even after the key was turned off. It provided transportation for me, my family and the other family member who purchased it a short time later. I was able to float a loan and purchase a good used vehicle. The loan process was not easy, but I saw God's love through the loan officer who took a chance on me, even though my credit was terrible.

Jerry's death was all over the front page of the newspapers, with pictures of the car he had died in, and I was furious. I remember being so angry. My sister drove by my house about the time I was leaving in the wee hours of the morning. She insisted on riding with me when I told her my plans to drive to the country store where the local newspaper was sold and buy all of them. I took a roll of quarters and bought every paper in the rack. I think they were only twenty-five cents at that time. Then I drove to another country store to buy all that had been delivered to that newspaper stand. I remember running out of quarters and stealing a few as it was based on the honor system.

I'm sure Maurita thought I had lost my mind as I drove to the bridge close to where I lived and threw them all in the river. It felt good watching them float down the river.

I was so convinced that Jerry did not take his own life as it had been printed in the newspapers. A short time later I composed a three-page letter to President Ronald Regan, with copies to senators and congressman and five newspapers, including the *Lexington Herald*. I took my frustrations out on the federal government because I felt they had let him down. I wanted people to know that Jerry led a normal childhood and was raised by a Christian family. I wanted them to know his death was not a mystery like the newspaper headlines had said. I explained how he served two tours in Vietnam and listed all his awards. I wanted people to know that he was in Vietnam when the so called cease-fire was initiated in January 1973. I wanted them to know how fifteen years later at the age of forty-three, he became another Vietnam War casualty. I felt like our nation would be judged for what happened to the Vietnam War veterans. I wanted people to know that the ones like Jerry, who survived, were as much casualties as the ones who lost their lives during the war. I wanted people to know Jerry loved God and his country. He was disappointed with the functions of the government and the Veterans Administration. Jerry felt the VA gave preference to alcoholics over those with PTSD. Instead of helping Jerry during the five weeks he was hospitalized in the psychiatric ward, Jerry could only see the horrible pain and suffering of his fellow veterans. He often told me he did not want to end up like many of them. He was a strong person and did not want his daily life to be controlled by drugs. He was scheduled to be admitted back in the VA a month before he died, but there were no beds available. He was advised not to stop taking the drug Xanax until he could be admitted into the hospital and be taken off it gradually. At the time of his death, he was still on the waiting list for a bed. I wrote the following on the last page of my letter:

> My prayer for you, Mr. President, is that you will help other Vietnam veterans and their families before it is too late for them. There are thousands of disturbed veterans out there and it is not too late to appropriate the necessary funds to help them. Since the President pushes for defense, the consequences of the conflicts caused by that needs to be backed up by the VA as mandated by Congress. Gerald L. Thomas lost a lot of battles since Vietnam but he finally won the war. He was a Christian and often spoke of how God was the only one who could help him. I know you probably will toss this letter aside and say, another one bites the dust. But I do know one thing for sure, when Jesus Christ returns He will establish the great government of God...A real functioning, all-powerful and divine government where every knee will bow to Him...And at last, the people of this tired, oppressed, polluted old world will have a government that is honest, fair, just and competent, with power to make it work.

I was amazed at the cards and letters I received from other veterans and their families who were going through the same thing I had been through. I received a letter from a veteran in prison who read my article in the paper and was very touched by it. He wanted me to know that my letter is doing someone somewhere some good. A retired sergeant from the USMC (United States Marine Corps) wrote me a letter thanking me for having the courage to say the things that I said as he too had experienced the same things Jerry did. He said my letter touched his heart, especially when I mentioned my husband's commitment to Christ. He said the only thing that helped him make the transition from Vietnam to any kind of peace was through a relationship with Jesus Christ. He prayed for God to give me grace and comfort. I even got a sympathy letter from the White House, as well as one from my US senator. One night I got a phone call from another veteran saying he had been thinking about taking his own life until he read my letter. He said it gave him hope knowing there were people out there who really cared. God was using my suffering to help others, and I thanked Him for that. Those cards and letters I received were what helped me get through my grief. I learned from that experience that God was with me. Jesus grieved with me. I finally stopped asking why and looking for answers. I took my pain and helped someone else through my letter to the president. I am grateful because I learned that God is worthy of my trust in Him.

Just when I thought things couldn't get any worse, I was audited by the IRS and my daughter Stefanie, who was home from college for one weekend, totaled my new vehicle on her way home from the movies with my younger daughter, Alison. I saw God's love through the Good Samaritan who brought my daughters home that cold night. I was so thankful they were not hurt when I drove to the accident scene the next morning and was amazed they had survived with only a few cuts and bruises. I was also amazed when I met with my loan officer to explain what had happened. I remember feeling relieved when he said not to worry, that it would look good on my credit report when it showed I had purchased a vehicle and paid it off within the same month. He asked me to fill out another loan application so I could purchase another vehicle. The loan was approved.

The girls and I made it fine the rest of the year in that old farmhouse. In the spring I found a part-time job managing apartments in Columbia near the bank where I worked full time. I worked for my rent. I had banker's hours and was able to go to the apartment complex where I lived and work from 4:00 to 6:00 p.m. I saw God's love through my friends and the people from church who helped me move from the old farmhouse to town. My daughter Alison got a job working at the Dairy Queen after school, and Stefanie dropped out of college for a semester and got a job working for a dentist. I was barely getting by financially, but by the grace of God, we made it.

5

Healing after Loss

Now that I'm retired, and life is good, I find myself getting up early, sometimes early enough to see the sun come up. My husband Tom is making a morning person out of me. He always gets up first and makes the coffee. There's nothing like waking up to the aroma of fresh coffee. I'll always be grateful for a fresh cup. There was a time in my life when I recycled coffee grounds from the day before because I did not have money to buy groceries till the end of the month, a time in my life when I was like a broken piece of pottery, trying to figure out how to put my life back together.

I reflected back on 1988, when I had just buried my second husband, Jerry, and how hard it was to make ends meet. I had two daughters to support, and my child support checks were coming few and far between. I was working as a bank teller and only got paid at the end of each month. I always had too much month left at the end of my money. The bank had a dress code, and we were required to wear panty hose and high-heeled shoes. We could wear pantsuits, as they were called. I remember wearing slacks toward the end of the month because I didn't have any panty hose without runs in them. Christmas was coming soon, so my daughter Alison and I stripped tobacco to earn enough money to remember the season of giving.

I learned what Paul meant in Philippians 4:12 (NIV) when he wrote, "I know what it is to be in need, and I know what it is to have plenty. I have learned the secret of being content in any and every situation, whether well fed or hungry, whether living in plenty or in want." God was teaching me and molding me way back then because He wanted me to become a woman of God who reflects the heart of Jesus. He knew my struggles were not over, and I had a lot of growing in my faith to become what He wanted me to be.

It's another Tuesday, and I joyfully walked into the nursing home humming "Have Thine Own Way, Lord." I stopped suddenly when I noticed there was no one seated out front. My first thought was, *Maybe they don't want me to play the piano today or any day.* I was relieved when the activity director met me in the hall and said they had quarantined everyone because of a virus. I was relieved as I turned to leave quickly, thinking I didn't want to catch it. I almost ran over a lady I had gotten to know over the years. She had joined our group and regularly visited her sister there. She said she felt guilty not seeing her sister today. I assured her that her sister would understand and told her how blessed her sister was to have her visit so faithfully, as many of the residents were not that fortunate. I took time to talk with her and hopefully cheer her up. I knew she had suffered the loss of her only son and was still grieving.

Since I had a whole extra hour of free time, I decided to go by the church early and drop off my card table before I went to the prayer room. Tom and I had signed up to take a marriage course at my church, and we were asked to bring our own table as we would be served a meal at our own romantic table for two. This would be the third marriage course we had taken since we exchanged our vows, less than two years ago, in the little country church I grew up in. We vowed then to always keep God in the center of our marriage. We both knew it takes a whole lot of effort to make a marriage work, especially with our blended families. We both felt like God brought us together at a time in our life when we needed each other. Tom also had suffered loss of a spouse. We both felt God had given us another chance for happiness in our retirement years. God is all about second chances. I was carrying my card table down the hall when I ran into Cindy, our connections minister, who introduced me to our worship director. He was telling her about the next sermon series, which would be called "Pieces: When Broken Becomes Beautiful." I immediately blurted out my thoughts, as I often do when I'm excited, interrupting their conversation, and told him that would be a great title for the book I'm writing. The worship director said, "I don't think it's taken. Go for it." I had been praying about what God wanted me to name my book. I couldn't wait to get to the prayer room and thank God for that moment. If I had stayed and played the piano at the nursing home, I would have missed out on that conversation. I knew that was God's timing. I stayed a little longer than usual as I had a lot to talk to Him about besides praying for those whose names had been dropped in the offering plate on Sunday. As I left the church, my burdens felt lighter, and the world seemed brighter as I felt God speaking to me through my church friends. I couldn't wait to get home and write some pages in my book.

I found a quiet place and sat down to write. My mind immediately went back to May of 2008 and how God got me through that muddy season in my life. I kept a journal entitled "Learning to Fall" the first year after Bobby's death. As part of my healing process, I recorded every detail. The funeral was really hard, but the days and weeks after the funeral were the hardest. Journaling was therapy for me, and I recorded my thoughts and what I was really going through. I read my Bible and prayed a lot. God seemed to send just the right people at just the right time when I was at my lowest point.

I was invited to take the Disciple 1 Bible Class on Wednesdays with some of the most awesome Christian people in our church. I looked forward to Wednesdays, when

I could spend two hours with people who loved Christ and loved me. I invited everyone to my house for the last session, where we had communion and celebrated our victory. I had planned on having everyone on my back porch, but it poured, and we had to move inside. Pastor Adam played my piano, and I remember asking him why my piano didn't sound like that when I played it. Joe Patterson was our class clown and made me laugh a lot. He is now our congregational care pastor and the leader of our Stephen Ministry. I've spent a lot of time praying for our Stephen Ministry these past few years, and Joe is one of those answered prayers.

The church sent me to Orlando, Florida, in January for a week's training to become a leader in our Stephen Ministry, which is such an important part of my life today. God knew January of 2009 would be hard for me, so He found something for me to do. God knew exactly what I needed and worked out the details while I was home grieving. I not only grieved the loss of my deceased husbands, Bobby and Jerry, I also grieved the loss of my parents and my divorce way back in 1987. I had never taken the time to grieve properly, and one must take the time to grieve. It is necessary because you can never heal what you can't feel.

My friends Larry and Sally took me out to eat and invited me to come visit Celebrate Recovery on Sunday nights. Larry was also leader of the Stephen Ministry program I was involved in at the time. Celebrate Recovery, also known as CR, is a Christ-based approach to recovery from all kinds of hurts and hang-ups. Celebrate Recovery utilizes eight recovery principles that are based on the Sermon on the Mount. At the time of Bobby's death, I was volunteering at church on Wednesdays, helping with the bulletins for the service, but I had no idea I'd be attending the service a short time later.

I came to CR for the first time full of grief, but I didn't realize until I had started working the program that I also had a bad case of codependency. I had been a codependent woman all my life because I allowed the behavior of another person to affect my behavior and became consumed with that person and their problem. A little bit of codependency can be good as the Bible tells us to put others first, but it also tells us to love others equal as ourselves and not more. I remember the first song the praise band sang that night titled "ICU" (a beautiful song meaning everywhere I look, I see God). I hated it because all I could think of was my husband dying in an intensive care unit a million miles away from home, and they wanted me to sing about it? Suddenly the tears began to flow, and I cried during the rest of the worship service. I told God if He would just let me get out of there, I'd be okay. That was one time God didn't answer my prayer the way I had asked. He knew my need better than me and had placed me exactly where I needed to be.

Two years later I stood before that group of people (some new and some who had journeyed with me through my grief and codependency) giving my testimony in hopes it would help someone else. I stepped out of my safe zone into my faith zone, knowing I was not a public speaker, and I leaned heavily on God to help me. I was dating Tom at that time and attending a small group he was teaching. He and his small group showed up that night and sat on the front row. My friends and family came, and that made me even more nervous. I feared saying something that might offend them. I wore the T-shirt my niece had given me that said, "I Pray" and the bracelet that had Philippians 4:6 on it for extra support. A favorite soloist sang "One Day at a Time," and the praise band sang "ICU." This time I listened to that song with a whole different perspective. I got it! Everywhere I looked, I saw God. I looked over that crowd of people and saw God, realizing my church was a hospital for sinners and CR was an intensive care unit for those who are hurting and seriously wounded. My testimony was a short *Reader's Digest* version of the book I'm writing today. I said in my closing statement, "Every morning I wake up and thank God for all the good and the bad I've been through. Loss has been a part of my journey. In spite of these happenings and perhaps because of them, I am becoming the person God has intended for me to be. I praise Him for continuing to love me and for opening new doors every day so that I can come to fully understand His love and purpose for me in this life. I am living in His glory at this very moment. My all-time favorite verse in the Bible is 1 Corinthians 13:13 (NIV) reads, 'And now these three things remain, faith, hope and love, but the greatest of these is love.' God has shown his love to me in so many ways and continues to do so today. He not only became my best friend, he sent other friends to be there for me and walk with me through my storm. When the rain finally stopped, I didn't have to wade through the mud alone to get where God wanted me to be. I learned through Celebrate Recovery that broken can become beautiful when grace sings the melody."

A little over a year after her son died, my dear sweet mother-in-law passed away, and more grief was dumped upon me like a gigantic hailstorm. She had been like a mother to me, especially since my mother died suddenly with an aneurysm at the age of seventy-one, only a few months after Bobby and I married. I sat there beside her at her son's funeral thinking no mother should have to bury their child. She kept asking why it couldn't have been her instead. At the age of eighty-seven, she felt she had led a good life and was so ready to go to heaven. I didn't have an answer for her, I just showed her love and prayed for God to give her strength. I thought about my own mother, who lost her first child at only thirteen months and how very hard it must have been for her. I remembered when I had a miscarriage and lost my first child and when my daughters both suffered the same way. I thought a lot about death and dying, but I tried not to dwell on it. Rather, I concentrated on the positive things that were all around me at that time.

I've learned through the muddy seasons of my life that if I put my trust in Christ, who came to set me free, and cast my burdens on Him, I don't have to be hurried or worried by the day's events. Ecclesiastes 3:1(NIV) is a scripture I memorized in high school: "There is a time for everything, and a season for every activity under heaven." God tells me to enjoy whatever season I'm in in my life. I have to remind myself daily that God commands me to get some rest and take care of myself. I can't be everything to everyone all the time. My codependency still kicks in every now and then, and I have to work on it. I read somewhere we must not confuse the command to love with the disease to please. God didn't rush to create the world; he followed it with a day of rest. God wants us to create, observe, enjoy, and then relax. He wants us to set priorities and boundaries so that we can enjoy every activity under heaven. I haven't completely been healed from my codependency and probably never will be, but at least I'm aware of it and am taking steps to control it. Prayer, Bible study, and singing old hymns like "I Don't Know about Tomorrow, But I Know Who Holds My Hand" helps me put everything in perspective and renew my faith in God.

It wasn't until I suffered great loss that I really studied the Bible. I grew up in church and always read my Bible, but I never really studied the Bible until I got involved in my ministries at church. I memorized John 3:16 (NIV) as a child and knew it by heart: "For God so loved the world that He gave His only son, that whoever believes in Him shall not perish but have eternal life." I just thought it meant I was assured I'd go to heaven someday. Today, I get the "so loved that he gave" part. God's Word is so full of His love.

It's a book about love. God's love is perfect and unfailing. When I learned to really trust in God's love, the healing and comfort began. On the days that I felt lonely and unloved and my emotions were running wild, I chose to take God at His Word and believe.

God showed His love through my forever friends, who invited me to go on vacation with them and tag along on New Year's Eve, even though I was the only one without a spouse or date. I saw God's love through my friend Jan, who invited me to spend a week at her condo in Vero Beach, Florida, with just five of us girls. I saw God's love through my friend and Pilates exercise instructor, who gave me some free exercise classes in memory of Bobby. I specifically remember Kathy sharing my testimony with the entire exercise class a few months later. She shared how she was touched by it. She later joined our church and brought another exercise friend with her. My small group prayed for me and with me when we met on Wednesdays at noon. I saw God's love through my forever friends from Adair County. Norma and Sammy and Marsha and Larry have been there for me over the years. Our kids grew up together, and we have kept in touch over the years. They were there for me when I went through my divorce. They were there to celebrate with me when I remarried and grieve with me when I buried two husbands. They were never judgmental, just loving and kind. That's why I call them my forever friends. I remember them coming back to the house after Bobby's funeral and Sammy telling me as he left that now would be a good time for me to write my book. I saw God's love through my neighbors, who not only brought comfort food to my house but were also there for me with the little things I needed help with. I thank God for my dear friend and neighbor who lives across the street, especially during the hot summer months when she invited me to her pool. I saw God's love through Pastor Rick and Pastor Adam as they encouraged me not only in their sermons, but when they took the extra time to say a kind word and give me a hug when I ran into them in the hallway at church. My fellow Stephen ministers and even those people at the nursing home where I played the piano on Tuesdays were there for me. I was surrounded by healthy Christians, those who took a daily dose of God's word and chose to believe it worked. I wanted to become a healthy Christian like them.

There was a time my kids were worried about me spending too much time grieving and talking about the past. They called my sister, who came and spent the night with me. I saw God's love through Maurita when she invited me to spend the weekend in the country with her and travel to parts of the four-hundred-mile yard sale across Kentucky. She not only cheered me up, she wore me out. She knew I needed a change of scenery and some physical exercise. I was suffering from the sin of unbelief. I think I had been through so much that I couldn't believe it had actually happened. It wasn't that I didn't believe in God. I was having trouble believing in myself. My kids posted two sayings on my kitchen wall for me to read every morning. One read, "One Day at a Time;" the other read, "Believe." I still read them every day to remind me that God is with me and loves me. It is my job to take life as it comes one day at a time and believe in God's unfailing love!

Another part of my healing began when I was asked by Pastor Adam to do an interview with him during a sermon he was preparing called "Closer Than You Think." My first reaction was to say no, but I prayed about it and knew God would be with me. Even though it had only been a year since Bobby died, I felt like I must share if it would inspire others to take steps to get closer to Christ. I remember waking up early that Sunday morning and feeling really nervous, especially when I got in my car to drive the short distance to church and found that the battery was dead. My first reaction was to call my daughter for a ride. I realized I could walk and be there by the time she drove to my house, so I started walking. I spent the entire ten minutes praying for strength, and by the time I arrived, I was actually calm.

I simply shared how God had been there for me through my friends and family. I had so many God stories I could tell, but I shared the one that warmed my heart the most. I talked about when my friend Elwood called me the Saturday after Bobby's funeral and asked if there was anything he could do for me. I told him he could go to church with me on Sunday and sit in Bobby's chair in the Cup of Hope, as I didn't think I could go and look at his empty chair. The worship service is simulcast to another room that is called the Cup of Hope.

This room is furnished with comfortable tables and chairs, sofas, and love seats. It simulates a coffee café. Many people who have disabilities or require special seating worship in the Cup of Hope. This was where Bobby and I worshiped every Sunday. Elwood and Donna were there and have been attending ever since.

I also shared how grateful I was to God and Pastor Rick, who preached a twenty-one-day series based on Philippians 4:6. It started three months after the day Bobby died. He gave out orange bracelets with "Worry Free" imprinted on them, and he challenged us to wear one and give ten away. I knew that was a sign from God for me to reach out and encourage someone else instead of staying home and crying and feeling sorry for myself. I was so inspired after the sermon on Sunday that I stopped at the welcome desk on my way out and took a handful. I took so many I later offered to pay for them. I gave them out to friends and family, as well as people at the post office. I mailed them, along with copies of Rick's sermon, to people I knew might be hurting or suffering. One day at a time, God was giving me the guidance I had prayed for. I was learning to take my mind off myself and on to others. I wrote in my journal there were three important lessons I learned that past year:

1. I was stronger than I ever imagined.
2. Jesus was closer than I realized.
3. I was loved more than I ever knew.

I learned what it meant to really put my faith and trust in God when the days of adversity were suddenly upon me. I learned everything is in God's perfect timing, even if we don't see it at the time. I stepped out of my safe zone when I said yes to God, but I was blessed more than I could imagine.

6

Listening to a Higher Power

Not long after Bobby died, I signed up for Disciple 1 Bible Class. I knew I was in good hands as Pastor Adam was our leader and some of my favorite church people were also signed up. They not only comforted me during my grieving process, but I learned from them and grew in my faith. I shared one day that I had been praying for God to speak to me about my purpose for life. I look back now and see He had been speaking to me all my life. I just hadn't been listening.

One rainy day when I was sitting alone in my big empty four-bedroom house, I decided I'd take a tour and invite Jesus to walk with me through every room. I felt God speaking to me that day as He told me what I needed to get rid of and what I needed to keep. Bobby had been such a pack rat and never threw anything away. I started sorting in piles of threes:

discard, share, and keep. He told me to make each bedroom God-friendly by leaving something in each room that guests and family might relate to. I thanked Him as I looked at the pictures on the wall of my two beautiful daughters and granddaughters and stepchildren, who had brought so much joy into my life. I looked at the way I had decorated the rooms and noticed the Love, Dream, Live poster I had placed over the old wrought iron bed. I felt God telling me I had a wonderful marriage with Bobby, but he would want me to be happy and move on with my life. I noticed the cross on the wall and the award clocks Bobby and I had each received. We were both voted Associate of the Year by our peers in the Builders Association, and the engraving on the clock read, "For Dedicated Service to This Association to the Building Industry and Having Given Unselfishly of Your Time Toward the Success of the Association—This is the highest honor the association can bestow on an associate member from the Building Association of Bowling Green." It reminded me that we were hard workers and deserved that award. I thought of the heavenly award Bobby had already gotten. I got excited thinking about how awesome my reward will be if I remain faithful and obedient until God calls me home. I smiled, and I remembered how proud and honored I was when I had accepted my award at the annual Christmas dinner and dance. I stopped and looked at the cross hanging on the wall in the hall near the bookcases I was about to tackle. God reminded me of the price he paid on that cross in Calvary so that I might receive my reward in heaven.

I started going through books that I thought Jesus might not approve of and tossed several in the discard pile. I felt Him telling me to get rid of any literature that was not helpful, pure, good, and true. I did not get any negative feedback from the pictures on the wall as God is all about family. There on the top shelf, I spotted the journals I had kept over the years. I sorted them by date and carefully placed them back on the shelf, thinking someday I'll refer back to them and write my book. Here I am six years later doing just that.

The next day I woke up to find another rainy day. I decided to continue my tour through the house and invited Jesus to go with me. I became uncomfortable when I opened the door to the attic, thinking maybe I won't ask Jesus to go here, but I'm glad I did. He and I spent most of the day in that attic going through old papers. My discard pile grew larger and larger. Jesus was there with me as I sat on a stool reading old divorce papers, old cancelled checks. Parts of it were painful, yet parts of it were joyful. Jesus laughed and cried with me when I found the first birthday card Bobby had given me. On the front was the most beautiful poem called "Desiderata." It was written by Max Ehrmann in 1927. I read aloud some of the lines. "Nurture strength of Spirit to shield you in sudden misfortune. Many fears are born of fatigue and loneliness. Keep peace with your soul. Be cheerful. Strive to be happy."

Going through all that stuff in the attic that day, I felt Jesus guiding my decisions on what to keep and what to throw away. I felt a sense of peace I had never felt in my life. The hardest part was when we went back downstairs to the master bedroom closet, where I still had several of Bobby's clothes hanging. I asked Jesus if we could wait another day, and He told me to take my time but to remember they were just clothes and Bobby didn't need them anymore. I later saw God's love through my sister-in-law, Judy, who came and helped me. I gave all his warm clothes to help the homeless in Nashville through my daughter's church. I also gave shoes and blankets, sweaters, and coats to a homeless person I found out about through my church. God seemed to guide and direct me as I continued to pray and trust. By the end of the week, I had enough in my discard pile to have a huge bonfire in the chiminea in my backyard. I warned my neighbors so they wouldn't call the fire department. I was on a mission. God reminded me that my house didn't hold memories, but my heart did. He reminded me to get rid of the bad and hang on to the good. "Get rid of excess baggage" became my motto for a while.

Looking back, I am thankful God gave me the strength to endure. I depended on Him, and He has given me the awesome privilege of watching Him work in my life through the difficult times. I did not understand at the time what God would accomplish through my trials, but I was sure He was working everything out for my good. My Disciple

1 Bible Class helped me stay focused on Jesus instead of my difficulties. He gave me hope and strength and motivated me to keep on going. I vowed that day that I would invite Jesus to go with me everywhere I went. There may be places I have taken him where he might not have wanted me to go, but He never deserted me, as he promises in Hebrews 13:5. If you are in tough times and begin to doubt, cling to this promise. Looking for God's presence in your life will allow you to hang on until the Lord gives you a victory or changes your circumstances. God has used my suffering to draw me closer to Him. When we learn to live wholeheartedly for the Lord, even in difficult times, others will see His life displayed in us. Isn't that what we were put on this earth to do? Live in a way that draws others to Christ? I am grateful that God is using my suffering and pain for His good purposes. He has shown me how much I need Him; therefore, I strive hard to walk obediently with Him and let His strength flow through me.

Reflecting back on September 1, 2009, which would have been mine and Bobby's nineteenth wedding anniversary, I saw God's love through a hibiscus plant I had on my back porch. I remember feeling sad when I woke up thinking I would never get flowers from him again. I had tried to save a beautiful hibiscus plant a friend had given me at Bobby's funeral. It bloomed beautifully all summer after his death and had lots of full blooms on our eighteenth wedding anniversary. I knew it was an annual plant, but I tried to save it by cutting it back, bringing it into my garage, and watering it all winter. I sat it back on my porch in the spring in hopes it would bloom again. By the end of August, my daughter, Alison, told me I might as well get rid of it as it wasn't going to bloom. I couldn't wait to call my daughter and tell her my hibiscus plant had the most beautiful bloom on it. The fact that it had its first bloom on our anniversary was a sign from God that my life was going to be beautiful again. I felt like Bobby was telling me he was in heaven, where the most beautiful flowers were blooming, and this was just a small sample of what heaven was like.

7

Powering Down to Power Up

I WOKE UP this morning with the sin of unbelief creeping back into my life. That's something I have to fight every day. We had a terrible storm last night, and the TV in my bedroom went out. I called the cable company, and they told me to "power down and power up," and of course it didn't work. I was on the phone with them for a long time and tried all the other things they told me to do. Finally, they said they would need to send a technician out, but not today.

My husband, Tom, didn't seem to be too concerned about it as he didn't think we should have a TV in the bedroom anyway. I didn't think much about it the rest of the day until bedtime. Not knowing how I could go to sleep without watching a little of the news or Hallmark Channel, I remembered I did have a DVD player that worked and found a movie titled *Crash*, starring Sandra Bullock and Matt Dillon. After watching the first ten minutes and listening to foul language and racist remarks, I knew this wasn't my kind of movie. Instead of turning it off, I told myself I'd just bleep out the bad language in my mind, and maybe it would get better. After watching another ten minutes, I realized it wasn't getting any better, so I turned it off. I couldn't go to sleep for thinking about all the violence I had just seen, so I immediately starting praying and thinking about the book I was trying to write. Evil thoughts from the enemy kept telling me I couldn't write a book, thoughts like, *What makes you think you can write a book?* and *Who would want to read about your crazy mixed-up life?* kept creeping into my head.

When I woke up the next morning, I still had those same evil thoughts, and I shared with Tom. He said, "That's not like you." I knew he was right, so I called the cable company again, and when they told me it would be almost a week before they could send someone out, I did not get upset but rather made the appointment. Hanging up the phone, I thought maybe God was trying to tell me something, like maybe I should take the TV out of the bedroom and forget it. I thought maybe it was God telling me I shouldn't write my story. I had been so worried about saying the wrong thing and offending someone. I picked up one of the books I had ordered on Amazon.com about writing a nonfiction book. I turned to the back cover and read, "If you've ever wondered if you could write a book, the answer is, yes, you can!" I read several inspirational pages and began to get my courage back. Besides my Bible, that little book became my guidebook.

Tom left to go play golf. I read my devotion, prayed, and laid out my writing material, as if to tell the devil I plan to write my book, and headed straight for the piano. My piano and I have been together since I was twelve years old. I sat down on the rickety old piano bench and just stared at the empty spaces between the notes. I sat there in silence, asking God to take away all my evil thoughts and forgive me for wasting my time last night watching the movie I had just thrown in the trash. I asked Him to fill me with the Holy Spirit and give me words of wisdom and strength to continue writing. The closest thing to God sometimes is silence. We must take the time to be still and know that He is God and then listen for his voice speaking to us. Just like music depends upon those empty spaces between the notes for its meaning, our words must have silence around them too, or they will lose their meaning. I opened an old country/ Western gospel hymnbook I had kept over the years and randomly came to a song called "Only Believe." I played and sang all the verses, my favorite being "Fear not little flock, He goeth ahead, your Shepherd selected the path you must tread. The waters of Marah He'll sweeten for thee. He drank all the bitter in Gethsemane. Only Believe, only Believe. All things are possible, only Believe." God spoke to me that day as clear as if He was sitting beside me on the piano stool. I heard Him tell me not to give up.

I walked into the kitchen just as the phone was ringing and read the words on a notepad lying there by the phone that said, "Watch your THOUGHTS; they become words. Watch your WORDS; they become ACTIONS. Watch your ACTIONS; they become HABITS. Watch your HABITS; they become CHARACTER. Watch your CHARACTER; it becomes your DESTINY." I answered the phone, and it was the cable company calling to tell me they had been able to repair my cable box and to please turn on the TV to see if it was working, and sure enough it was. I noticed the sign over my stove in the kitchen that said, "Believe." I felt God telling me to continue writing my book one word at a time and believe in His awesome power to work out all the details. All I had to do was just stop every now and then to power down and power up. All I had to do was to put forth the effort and believe and listen through the Holy Spirit, which had taken up residence again in my heart. I was able to sit down, and the words just seemed to flow across the page. I told myself, "I can do all things through Christ who strengthens me." I had no idea that all those years of journaling could one day be used to glorify God. I did it because I enjoyed it. It was healing and comforting, like playing the piano.

Most writers have to travel to a site or place they are writing about. Not me. The longest distance I have traveled so far has been to the local library, where I checked out some books on how to begin writing. I felt God guiding me in the right direction on Monday after I had accepted Pastor Rick's challenge during his sermon called "Driven: The Road to the Good Life." It was about setting goals that guide. He asked us to set a goal, a personal or spiritual goal. He said God's number 1 goal is to shape us to be more like His Son. Inserted in the bulletin was a Thomas Menton prayer, which read,

> My Lord God I have no idea where I am going. I do not see the road ahead of me. I cannot know for certain where it will end. Nor do I really know myself, and the fact that I think I am following your will does not mean that I am actually doing so. But I believe that my desire to please you does in fact please you. And I hope that I have that desire in all that I am doing. I hope that I will never do anything apart from that desire. And I know that if I do this you will lead me by the right road though I may know nothing about it. Therefore will I trust you always though I may seem to be lost and in the shadow of death, I will not fear, for you are ever with me, and you will never leave me to face my perils alone.

I sure did need to read that this morning, and writing it down has changed my whole attitude about achieving my goal.

Pastor Rick asked us to stand up after we prayed this prayer if we had a goal in mind. I immediately thought how I'd had a dream about writing my story and perhaps having it published, which I had pushed on the back burner for a long time. I felt God nudging me and saying, "Now's the time."

So I stood up, thinking that with God's help, I could do this and possibly donate any proceeds from the sale of the book to a worthy cause. I shared it with Tom after we got home from church, and he suggested I give any proceeds to the new vision Pastor Rick spoke about in his sermon about starting a preschool for the underprivileged children in our community at the Foundry. That was my first sign from God telling me if I stayed focused on Him and wrote for all the right reasons and not to glorify myself in anyway, I'd be successful. I prayed about it all weekend, realizing what a big commitment I had made. I didn't know where or how to get started. I knew I had stepped way out of my comfort zone.

The following Monday afternoon when I picked up my granddaughter from school, I asked her if she wanted to stop for ice cream or go to the library. When she said, "Let's go to the library," I knew that must be another sign from God. I saw God through my granddaughter Ann-Riley as she helped me pick out books on how to get started on writing. It was Ann-Riley who chose to go the library instead of Baskin-Robbins and Ann-Riley who led me upstairs and helped me pick out four books that have been very helpful to me. My favorite book was titled *I Have the Right to Write*. I felt God telling me to write words that were inspiring to others and share them with love. He told me to speak the truth in love.

As we were checking out, the gentleman at the desk noticed the book titles and asked if I would be interested in attending a free writing workshop on Saturday. I said, "Sure," and signed up without even asking who the speaker was. I just felt God leading me in the right direction to help me get started on reaching my new goal. It turned out to be a Southern writer. I had never heard of him, nor had I read any of his books; however, I went away from that three-hour workshop feeling good about writing and believing in my ability to reach my goal. I felt God guiding my arthritic fingers as I started to write from my heart. I felt inspired by God. I couldn't wait to get home and start writing. I prayed that night, believing without a shadow of a doubt that God would make a way for me. James 1:6 (NIV) says, "But when you ask, you must believe and not doubt, because the one who doubts is like the wave on the sea, blown and tossed by the wind."

I remember getting up the next morning and being passionate about starting to write my story. I began searching for old journals, scrapbooks, poems, and articles I had written and accumulated over the years. I came across an Advent Devotion booklet that had been composed by members of my church. As I was thumbing through the pages, I came across the story I had written. It reminded me of the time when I had shared this very same devotional guide with quite an unexpected audience. This was during the time when I was seeking direction and purpose in my life. I remember stopping by the church to pick up an extra copy of the Advent Devotion to share with someone else. While taking a shortcut on my way to run an errand, I was stopped in the middle of the road by a service truck. I sat there for several minutes before I glanced over my left shoulder and noticed a nursing home. Thinking I might be stuck for some time, I picked up the extra copy of the devotion booklet and started reading it. I felt God telling me to pull into the parking lot of that nursing home and leave the copy I had of that little devotion booklet in the lobby of the nursing home, so I parked my car and planned to sneak in and sneak out without anyone noticing me. Just as I was laying the booklet on the table and getting ready to leave, I was approached by a volunteer who was there sharing God's love with them. He insisted I get up and read my story to the residents. I couldn't say no as I looked at the faces of those old folks who smiled to make me feel so welcome. Since it was early December and close to Christmas, I felt comfortable sharing the story I had written called "The Christmas Spirit." I read the scripture from John 4:23–24: "Yet a time is coming and has now come when the true worshipers will worship the Father in spirit and truth, for they are the kind of worshipers the Father seeks. God is spirit, and his worshipers must worship in spirit and in truth."

I shared with them a little bit of my story and how Christmas was going to be sad for me because this would be my second Christmas without my husband Bobby. Then I started to read aloud the following story:

> The first Christmas after my husband passed away, I was having a really hard time getting into the Christmas spirit; however I was determined to carry

on the normal family traditions. It was my husband who had always picked up two pies from his favorite local restaurant, so I did it. When I went to pick them up, I broke down and cried. I prayed all the way home for God to give me strength to get through the holidays.

I drove into the garage and quickly sat the pies on the counter where they always sat until time to serve them on Christmas Day. Hanging on the wall above the counter was my husband's coca-cola clock. It kept the correct time, but the light had burned out years ago. Just as I plopped those "stupid pies" (I called them at the time) on the counter, the clock lit up and shined brightly all through Christmas and is still shining brightly today. Standing there in the garage weeping over those two pies, I suddenly felt the presence of God reminding me to be patient; to wait on Him and everything would be okay. I attended the candlelight service at church on Christmas Eve and worshipped God in spirit and in truth, thanking Him for His love and the miracle of Jesus' birth.

I closed with this prayer: "Lord, be with those who have lost loved ones this holiday season. May the Spirit of Christ comfort, strengthen, and heal us. In Jesus's name, amen." I also shared the following thought for the day: "Just because you lose someone doesn't mean that you stop loving them or they stop loving you."

When I had finished reading the story from the Advent Devotion booklet to the residents of the nursing home that day, Reverend Jessie insisted I play the piano and sing praises to God with them. It just seemed right, and I've been going back every week for the past six years.

The Coca-Cola clock story reminds me of the power of God. When the storms of life come along and shut us down completely, I know a Man who can inspire and invigorate us and power us up again. His name is Jesus, and if we turn to Him during our power outages and ask for wisdom and insight and strength, He will restore us and make us whole again. He makes us even better than we were before. I look back now and see how God saw the big picture of my life and how He was starting to put the broken pieces of my life back together like a jigsaw puzzle when He blocked the road with a delivery truck and nudged me to take that Advent Devotion booklet into the nursing home.

8

Becoming Something Beautiful

IT IS A beautiful fall crisp morning in September. *Today is going to be a good day*, I thought as I drove to a nearby restaurant to meet with my care receiver. I read my daily devotion and the scripture for today was from Philippians 2:13 (NIV): "For it is God who works in you to will and to act in order to fulfill his good purpose." I was fulfilling the purpose that God had called me to do several years ago when I trained to become a Stephen minister through my church. I was giving an hour a week of my time to be a caring Christian friend to someone who was hurting. I prayed that God would give me the right words to encourage my friend and let me know when to remain silent and listen. I prayed that she would see God's love in me.

I was on a mission for my Lord. I remembered how God had been so faithful when I went through a crisis and needed a shoulder to cry on. I felt God calling me to become a Stephen minister at one of the busiest times in my life. He works like that sometimes I think because you may need to give up something to serve Him. Following Jesus is not easy, but it is the only way to lead a joyful life. I knew it was a big commitment, but I also felt in my heart it was something I needed to do, so I signed up for fifty hours of training and have never regretted it.

The Stephen Ministry was begun in 1975 by a pastor in St. Louis who wanted to increase caregiving in his congregation. The ministry is now in place in thousands of churches of more than one hundred denominations. The service is provided at no cost. I am honored to be a part of it through my local church. Whether it be a divorce, the death of a loved one, the loss of job, or moving to a new place, we all face times of transition. I learned so much during that training course. I learned how to be a good listener. Most people going through a tough time don't want advice; they simply want someone to listen. I learned that firsthand after my husband died in 2008. I had been on the caregiving side of the ministry for three years, but suddenly I found myself on the receiving end. I found myself alone for the first time in my life. My kids were grown, with families of their own. I had spent most of my life being someone's wife, mother, and caregiver. I felt lost, not knowing what I was supposed to do with the rest of my life, thinking I couldn't survive in this big old empty house all by myself. My fellow Stephen ministers helped me see that I was not alone. They not only comforted me, prayed for me, and grieved with me, they walked beside me.

I'm amazed how God is using a little old country girl like me to lead our local Stephen Ministry. I never thought of myself as a leader, but when I said yes to God, He transformed my life into a remarkable journey. He has blessed me with joy and purpose beyond my wildest expectations. It's amazing what God can do with your life if you step out in faith and let Him lead you to where He wants you to be.

A favorite book I like to read to my grandchildren is *Oh, the Places You'll Go* by Dr. Seuss. It's such a joyous ode to life about believing in yourself as you go out into the world. I often read it even when my grandkids aren't around. I love to read phrases like "You're off to Great Places! Today is your day! Your mountain is waiting, so…Get on your way!" Yes, God spoke to me through Dr. Seuss when I read, "You have brains in your head. You have feet in your shoes. You can steer yourself any direction you choose. You're on your own. And you know what you know. And you are the one who'll decide where you go." I like to change it to "God and You together will decide where you go." God is the author of my story, and He has already written the final chapter.

I realized today as I listened to my care receiver share what was going on in her life that I was doing just what God wanted me to do.

> Jesus taught them many things by parables, and in his teaching said: "Listen! A farmer went out to sow his seed." (Mark 4:2–3, NIV)

I was simply being a caring Christian friend to someone in need of God's grace and love. I was simply being a good listener. I was sowing seeds of kindness. I especially felt God using me when she said she would never forget me telling her my story about the old yellow station wagon. I had shared with her about a time in my life when I went through a similar situation she was in, finding myself without a vehicle to drive.

My second husband, Jerry, was found dead in the trunk of our car seven days after he left home one stormy night to put air in a low tire. I never saw him again. I got $300 cash for the car motor, and even though it was back in 1988, you couldn't buy a car for $300. I bummed a ride with my sister to work for several weeks till one day I received a phone call from a friend who gave me an old yellow station wagon. He told me all I had to do was buy tires and a battery and it should run fine. He told me I'd be doing him a favor if I'd come get it out of his yard as he was tired of mowing around it. My kids and I still laugh about how it kept on running after I turned the key off. My daughter would ask me to not turn the key off when I dropped her off at school for fear of embarrassing her in front of her friends.

As we laughed about that old yellow station wagon, my care receiver said she sees how God took care of me and my kids. We all turned out okay, and that gives her hope. As we walked to our cars together after our meeting, she pointed to the car a friend of her dad's had sold her for $1 and said, "I've nicknamed my car old yellow." I thanked God for using me as I got into my 2004 Lexus, and drove home. I sat down at my piano and played an old song I played and sang a lot a few years back when I felt God calling me to become a Stephen minister called "Jesus Use Me."

It goes like this:

> Dear Lord I'll be a witness, if you will help my weakness. I know I'm not worthy Lord of Thee. By eyes of faith I see Thee upon the cross of Calvary. Dear Lord I cry, let me Thy servant be...Jesus use me, and Lord don't refuse me, for surely there's a work that I can do. And even though it's humble, help my will to crumble...Though the cost be great, I'll work for you.

I survived hard times because I chose not to quit and never give up on God. Many times I gave out, but God carried me when I couldn't make it on my own. I depended on God, and I saw His love through the wonderful Beard family who gave me that old yellow station wagon. God's promise in Genesis 28:15a (NIV) still stands today: "I am with you and will watch over you wherever you go." If you are struggling today, swallow your pride and ask God to help you. You will get through it. Asking for help is a sign of strength, not weakness. Matthew 18:20 (KJV) says, "For where two or three are gathered together in my name, I am there in the midst of them." God was there with me and my care receiver today as we prayed for strength and wisdom and guidance. Reach out for help and let others pray for you. It makes all the difference in the world.

When life stinks, God says, "Lean on Me." Hardships forces us to look upward. God promises in his word at the right time, in God's hands, something good will eventually come out of our suffering. It takes courage, which comes from a heart that is convinced that it is loved. I know God loves me because He has taken my scars and turned them into stars for his glory. He has given me purpose for my pain and a joyful heart to fulfill my purpose. God tells me in Proverbs 17:22a (ESV), "A Joyful heart is good medicine." In the Bible, there are 545 references to joy, merriment, happiness, laughing and rejoicing. Only 158 verses talk about sorrow. Joy is a choice. I try to celebrate God all day every day like it says in Philippians 4:4 (NIV): "Rejoice in the Lord always. I say it again, Rejoice!" Psalm 150:6 (KJV) says, "Let everything that has breath praise the Lord," and Proverbs 15:15 (MSG) says, "A miserable heart makes a miserable life; a cheerful heart fills the day with song." Don't you just love that scripture?

Life is full of pain and misery, which is all the more reason to keep God in our lives every day. If I didn't have God in my life, I couldn't survive. I know where I've been, but only God knows where I'm going. "Grief can take care of itself, but to get the full value of joy you must have somebody to divide it with" is a favorite quote of mine by Mark Twain. Perhaps that is why God has blessed me with four husbands. Most people who don't know my story are shocked when they find out I've been married four times. I just laugh and say, "Yes, but none of them were my fault." I used to be embarrassed and didn't want anyone to know my past, but now I see my greatest ministry has come through my pain.

My life story has many chapters. One bad chapter doesn't mean it's the end of my book. "But those who wait on the Lord shall renew their strength: They shall mount up with wings like eagles, they shall run and not be weary. They shall walk and not faint." Isaiah 40:31 (NKJV) tells me to be patient and wait on the Lord. I thank God that my past doesn't define me and that the sacrifice of his son, Jesus, does. Reflecting on my journals as I continue to write is a great reminder that it was because of His mercies that I survived my situations. It strengthens my faith as I see how God prepared me ahead of time for what I was facing. I thank God for my personal growth through in-depth Bible studies and for the knowledge He gave me of His truth to survive. I have learned through my suffering that God is in control and that He will provide.

Serving God through the Stephen Ministry is the most awesome thing I can do. The more I fill my life with God and reach out to other people, the happier I become. The more I study God's word and live out those words, the more beautifully His love can be revealed through my actions. I am becoming more like Jesus. I am not where I want to be, but I thank God I'm not where I used to be. "But seek ye first The Kingdom of God, and his righteousness; and these things shall be added unto you." In Matthew 6:33 (KJV) is a scripture that helps me when fear and doubt starts creeping into my life.

9

Stepping Out in Faith

IN APRIL 2010, my church launched a three-year capital campaign with the goal of ensuring the long-term financial health of our congregation, positioning ourselves to capture the future God had for us. We were asked to pledge over and above our tithe for the next three years. I remember thinking it was not a good time for me to give more than I had already pledged. When my husband Bobby died, my income went down. Instead of decreasing my pledge, I upped it, believing God would take care of my needs. I was a retired widow pretty much relying on social security income.

This was a very difficult period of my life. I had suffered a substantial financial loss. Bobby and I had had virtually invested our life savings into our business. We sold the business a little over a year before Bobby passed away. The terms and conditions of the sale consisted of a promissory note and handshake agreement to be paid off in five years. The buyer was a personal friend of ours who came by the house to ask me if could sing a song that he had selected called "What a Day That Will Be" at Bobby's funeral. I graciously agreed and arranged it with the funeral director. I remember sharing with the buyer that day how blessed I felt not having to go back to work and run a business.

The buyer placed the company in bankruptcy a couple years after Bobby died after making only one payment, and I lost it all. In excess of 90 percent of the promissory note was unpaid and was written off in full during the bankruptcy process by the courts. I spent a lot of time praying and seeking godly counsel before I chose to turn it over to God and not file a lawsuit.

Reflecting on the Wednesday I met with my small group, who prayed with me and helped relieve my fears about meeting with my attorney that same afternoon, I feel certain I made the right decision. I felt God speaking to me that day through the scripture verses we were studying from the book of Ephesians. I was asked to read Ephesians 5:6–7 (NIV): "Let no one deceive you with empty words, for because of such things God's wrath comes on those who are disobedient. Therefore do not be partners with them."

I went to my attorney's office with my Bible in hand and told him I already knew what I needed to do. I told him I was not throwing what little money I had left away in a lawsuit.

He agreed with me and asked if I would share that scripture with him as he might like to use it with future clients.

I was working in the church office the following Monday when I turned in my pledge. My small group was studying a book by Sheila Walsh called *Beautiful Things Happen When a Woman Trusts God*. I stepped out in faith, trusting that God would supply all my needs and make a way for me to pay off my pledge in three years. I stopped concentrating on where I had been and where I was going and started focusing on who I was becoming in the process. I wanted to become more like Jesus. I shared in the celebration story two years later. "Through my giving to the As One campaign, I learned the true meaning of trusting God 100 percent, not just sometimes, but all the time. God has blessed me in the most amazing ways these past two years, not only financially, but spiritually and personally. I was even able to pay off my three-year pledge early. My life is not perfect, but I am where I am today in my faith journey by the grace of God and the fact that I chose to step out in faith and give."

Our church campaign finished strong and opened possibilities for new ministries as we freed up significant resources that are now no longer needed for debt service.

Soon after I wrote my first check, I inherited some money I had no idea I would be getting from my late husband's estate. My attorney told me how it came about was very unusual. I remember smiling and thanking God for blessing me so, and that is where I got the money to install new hardwood flooring. Every time I mop my shiny new floors, I praise God for allowing me to enjoy them. My piano even sounds better on the wood floors than it did on the old carpet. Just like me, it has more joyful sounds and plays a different tune, a tune that is more distinct and clear. My sister gave me a sign for my piano years ago that reads, "Life is like a piano, what you get out of it depends on how you play it." That same little quote is also on the piano at the nursing home, and I smile every time I read it.

When I was suffering, I increased my prayer life and the time I spent reading God's word. I learned to practice a steadfast mind when the world came crashing in on me. I had two choices—to worry or to pray. I chose to pray instead of worry. I depended on God for guidance. I allowed God to cleanse my heart and clear my mind. This is something I must do on a daily basis in order to experience joy in my life. I believe the wonders God wants to do in my tomorrows are prepared for me in my todays. Just like I have to keep my piano tuned in order for it to sound its best, I have to keep my life tuned in order for me to do my best for God and His kingdom here on earth. When singing, I sometimes get off-key when I hit the wrong note on the piano, but when I stop and start over and play the right note, my singing sounds better. God is the secret to keeping my life in tune so that I can fulfill His purpose for my life. I asked God to please stop all the losses in my life and give me joy. I read a scripture that says, "Serve the Lord with Joy, It's a delight to be in the will of God." Job 36:11 (NIV) says, "If they obey and serve him, they will spend the rest of their days in prosperity and their years in contentment." Luke 6:38 (NIV) says, "Give and it will be given to you. They will pour into your lap a good measure pressed down, shaken together and running over. For by your standard of measure it will be measured to you in return." I was blessed when I chose to step out in faith and give to the As One campaign.

I loved reading the gospel of Luke during the time I was striving to become more like Jesus. Luke didn't aspire to greatness. His goal in life was to serve and care for others. He too wanted to be like Jesus. Luke's stories about Jesus focused on his relationship with individual people, like we do in the Stephen Ministry. Jesus paid special attention to people who were ignored in society. He cared deeply for suffering and downtrodden people. Jesus offered salvation, strength, and healing to everyone he met. That's not always easy to do. Jesus was all about love, grace, and forgiveness.

I learned from my financial loss to trust in God, and I chose to forgive. I had a meeting with the person who bought our business and defaulted on the loan. I chose to forgive him. I put myself in the buyer's place and told him I'd rather be in my shoes than his. At least I wasn't the one who might be losing my home. I started concentrating on what I had instead of focusing on my loss. I opted to pray for him and his family and put it in my "something for God to do" box since it was out of my control. I have continued to use that little box over the years. I look back and am amazed how God took care of all those prayer requests I trustingly placed there. There's something magical about writing my prayer on a three-by-five card, knowing it's in good hands and waiting on the Lord. This process reminds me of when I was a kid making a Christmas list for Santa and being pleasantly surprised on Christmas morning. When life happens to deliver a situation to me that I cannot handle, I do not attempt to resolve it myself. I kindly put it in the "something for God to do" box. God will get to it in His time. All situations will be resolved in His time, not mine. God's timing is always right. God always does the right thing at the right time! Hebrews 4:16 (KJV) encourages us to "Let us come boldly unto the throne of grace, that we may obtain mercy, and find grace to help in time of need." When I place my written cares and concerns in that little box, it's like placing my burdens at the foot of the cross. It allows me to release my fears as I turn them over to God. Fear comes from uncertainty. Releasing my fears keeps me in my faith zone.

In the days and months after I surrendered my burdens to Christ, God gave me clarity on how to live my life. He tells us in Matthew 6:3 (NIV), "So don't worry about tomorrow, for tomorrow will bring its own worries. Today's trouble is enough for today." Sometimes I take the time to write God a thank-you note and place it in my box. I pulled one out today that reads, "Lord Jesus, thank you for every person that you have brought into my life. I know that you have a purpose for me with each of them. May I be to them what you want me to be." I have learned over the years that God doesn't always give you people you want. He gives you the people you need—the persons to help you, hurt you, leave you, love you, and make you the person you were meant to be.

God has been busy these past few years putting the broken pieces of my life back together. Why? Because I asked Him. It took me years to be able to turn it all over to Him. Sometimes I have to surrender one thing at a time, and I have to do it every day; otherwise, I wouldn't experience the joy I feel today. Faith and joy go hand in hand. Many times I give it up to God and take it back. When I find myself worrying and fretting, I give it back to Him. I still have issues I haven't completely turned over to God, but I'm aware of them, and I am working on them. It's not that I don't trust God to take care of them, I just don't want to lose control of them. Too bad we can't just surrender it all to Him at one time and be done with it. I am so aware of how life is subject to change every day. When I was contemplating marrying Tom, the devil crept into my life by telling me it wasn't going to happen. He worked through family members who tried to discourage me. He knew Tom was a strong Christian, and together we could make a difference for God's kingdom. It wasn't until I surrendered it over to God and placed a prayer in my "something for God to do" box that God showed me signs that we should be together. We consulted with three different pastors, but it wasn't until we turned it over to God that it came to be. I remember writing on a prayer request and dropping it in the offering plate one Sunday when Pastor Rick asked us to surrender all. I left church that day with a sense of peace, knowing God would work it all out. The only reason I have joy in my life today with Tom is because we included in our wedding vows to put God first and keep Him at the center of our lives. We meant them and are doing our best to live them. God is first and is the inspiration behind every good thing that we do. I'm thankful as I continue to write my story that I had the courage to let God work it out in his timing, not mine; otherwise, I'd still be a grieving widow sitting alone in the church pew on Sunday morning. God knew all along what was best for me, and He began working on putting the pieces of my broken heart back together when He healed the relationship with me and my family. God gave me another extended family to open my heart and home to. I had this big house, and Tom had two adopted children who had lost the only mother they ever knew and needed a motherly influence in their lives. God knew I knew from experience what it takes to blend families together, and with God's help, I see good things happening in Holly and Brant's lives. I give God all the credit. He gave me the skills and love to make it work.

The first Christmas after we married, I tried really hard to make it special for everyone. I knew that Bobby's kids and grandchildren were still grieving the loss of their dad and grandfather, and it was hard for them to come back home with him not there, let alone see me married to someone else. I knew it would be really hard for Bobby's grandkids. My heart was hurting for Brooke, Sarah, and Ethan when they first met Tom. I knew it would be hard for my kids and Tom's kids as well. It wasn't until I realized I couldn't please everyone and that the only person I had to please was God that I felt peace. I prayed for God to keep on reminding me that He was the director of my life. I prayed for faith to let Him plan my future. I asked Him to help me not worry about the parts other people were playing, especially when they were trying to direct my life. I prayed that He would show me what He wanted me to do and give me the courage to do it, and 1 Peter 5:7 (NIV) told me to "cast all your anxiety on God, because He cares for you." He said "all your anxiety," not "some of your anxiety." I believed, and He came through. I had to do my part for Him while He was working on my behalf. I tried to live my life in such a way that those who knew me but didn't know God might come to know God through me. I prayed every day, and still do, that someone would see God's love in me. I am working on a lifelong goal that no one ever reaches until eternity. The apostle Paul expressed in Philippians 3:12–14 (NLT), "I don't mean to say I have already achieved these things or that I have already reached perfection. But I press on to possess that perfection for which Christ first possessed me. No dear brothers and sisters, I have not achieved it, but I focus on one thing. Forgetting the past and looking forward to what lies ahead, I press on to reach the end of the race and receive the heavenly prize for which God, through Christ Jesus is calling us." I have a lot of character defects that only God can remove. Perfection only belongs to God. He knows my weaknesses and He will help me remove them if I let Him. True joy can be found in every situation of life when we recognize that God is at work and always in control. It is possible to act calm in painful and difficult times. Peace and joy come when we focus on things that provide lasting value to our life. The more I commit myself to knowing God's will through prayer and study of His word, the more prepared I am to help myself and others in our faith journey.

10

Choosing Joy

OH HAPPY DAY! I woke up this morning singing, "Oh Happy Day, when Jesus washed my sins away. He taught me how to watch and pray, and live rejoicing every day; Happy Day, Happy Day, when Jesus washed my sins away." I was about to witness my seven-year-old granddaughter being baptized. I sat there with twelve other family members anxiously awaiting the moment. It was one of the happiest moments of my life, and I was thanking God for allowing me to be there. I thought back to my childhood one hot July night when I was baptized at the age of twelve. I accepted Christ as my Savior during a revival meeting. The whole congregation traveled along a dusty gravel road to a nearby creek immediately after the service. It was dark, so the only light came from the moon and the headlights of the cars parked alongside the creek bank. I remember everyone singing "Shall We Gather at the River" as Brother Prince led me into the cold water and "O Happy Day" when we walked out of the water. I look back over the years as I continue to write my story for God's glory at how God has kept his promise to me. I wrote in my granddaughter's journal: "I know God is smiling down on you today. He is singing and rejoicing with shouts of joy. He is so proud of you, and so am I. He will celebrate the good times and grieve with you during the bad times and be with you all the days of your life. You can count on it 'cause you are now a child of God!"

I was blessed to have two Christian grandmothers who greatly influenced my life. Mama Jones, who lived to be ninety-eight, shared with me over the years a lot of wisdom that I wish I had written down. "Always remember, your reputation is something no one can ever take away from you" was one that I never forgot. I think God gives us a second chance with our grandchildren to correct all the mistakes we made raising our own children. I pray that I can pass down some good traits to my children and grandchildren so that God will use them to impact the world. Sometimes God's plan spans more than one generation. I don't know if I'll be able to finish this book. God may have put something in me bigger than I can accomplish, but I wouldn't be surprised if Ann-Riley finishes it for me someday if that is the case. I gave her a Christian journal, and I noticed she has already written about the day she was baptized on the first page. Perhaps

I've instilled in her the importance of journaling and can leave my family a legacy of some good things. I don't worry about leaving my family a lot of money. I want my life to speak words like *determination, persistence, integrity, godliness, generosity, favor, faith*, and *victory* to them. Before I was born, God gave me gifts and talents that were uniquely designed for me. It has taken me a long time to use some of them, but I feel I'm on the right track.

My small group is studying a book about joy. I was given the opportunity to facilitate the first chapter. The author believes joy is a choice and that the level of joy you experience is completely and totally up to you. Years ago when my friend Christine invited me to join her small group, I never imagined I would someday be facilitating the large group we have become today. We almost have enough to start our own church. I can't emphasize enough how this group of ladies has made an impact on my life and faith journey. We are a nondenominational group and have learned so much from one another.

When my late husband Bobby died, I saw God's love through my support group as they continued to pray for me and grieve with me. I was touched when they gave me a gift certificate for a massage at a health spa. They encouraged me when I was facing a financial crisis and helped me seek guidance through the scripture. When I announced I was contemplating marrying Tom, they encouraged me and prayed for me.

I opened the class today by telling my God friends my personal joy story and shared the following with them: "Over three years ago I came to class on Wednesday, and one of the members brought each of us cups with a scripture on it and asked us to pick one at random. My cup had the word *joy* written on it, and the scripture printed beneath it was from John 16:24: 'Ask using my name, and you will have Abundant Joy.'" I was so excited and shared how I felt God had chosen that cup just for me. I explained how I had been asking God to bring some joy into my life. I told God I was tired of grieving and feeling lonely. I asked Him to send a Christian man into my life. I told God I didn't want to marry again. I wanted companionship. I was working part-time at the church office, and Tom was also working there as a part-time custodian. I knew he was a Christian man, but I didn't know much else about his personal life. I had no idea he was a widower or if he was the least bit interested in me. I used Tom as an example of the kind of man I was looking for. The following week Tom called me and asked me to ride to Lexington, Kentucky, with him to hear his daughter sing in an opera at the University of Kentucky. It didn't dawn on me till after we hung up the phone that might be God answering my prayer.

Our first date was wonderful and the beginning of the life we now share together. On Monday morning I couldn't wait to share with some of the staff at work about how I had prayed for God to send me a Christian man and used Tom for an example. I further explained by telling them God had to show off and send Tom himself.

Shortly before Tom and I were to be married, Tom had a cancer scare. Once again, my small group and church family prayed us through. He got a clean bill of health on his next doctor visit. I learned what it meant to pray without ceasing like it says in 1 Thessalonians 5:17. To pray without ceasing is to keep your thoughts constantly filled with God, to keep your mind focused on God. It doesn't mean you have to pray all the time, twenty-four hours a day. No one can do that. It has been said that prayer is the greatest power in the universe. Spiritual power can change people's lives and the life of the world. When I started filling my mind and minutes with God, all of a sudden when I least expected it, marvelous things started happening to me. It was the result of praying and telling God what I needed. I starting praying boldly and specifically, believing that God would answer my prayer. Romans 12:12 (NIV) tells us to "be joyful in hope, patient in affliction, faithful in prayer." Prayer is the way to life itself.

Sometimes joy comes when you least expect it. I was doing some remodeling and having hardwood flooring installed. The contractor had to do a lot of sanding, which made a terrible mess. I had to move all my downstairs furniture to the sunroom, including my piano. I sat down one morning and wrote a song. It was during the time I was dating Tom. I had been looking up scriptures about joy and came across Ecclesiastes 2:26 (NLT): "God gives wisdom, knowledge, and joy to those who please him. But if a sinner becomes wealthy, God takes the wealth away and gives it to those who please him. This, too, is meaningless like chasing the wind."

I sat down at the piano and started singing, "For the one who pleases God, He gives wisdom, knowledge, and joy." I read the entire book of Ecclesiastes and found the secret to finding true joy and continued to finish my song. I wrote the words to remind myself how to have true joy. I played and sang it for Tom, and he thinks I should have it published someday. I learned life is God's good gift to be enjoyed responsibly, not a puzzle that must be solved. God spoke to me that day through the words of Solomon. He gave me the secret to living a joyful life. He told me to do things God's way, which in turn would lead to harmony with God, other people, and the world I'm living in. He told me if I trusted God and obeyed his plan for my life, I would live a productive and joyful life. He told me I would never understand why things that didn't make sense happened to me. He told me to celebrate the beauty of God's gift of life and its simple pleasures.

I was worrying about money at that time, thinking maybe I shouldn't spend money to have my floors replaced. Solomon also told me God never intended for me to live for my possessions and that I needed to make my relationship with God and others my primary concern. I had recently inherited some money and had given God his part first, so I felt like it was okay. Even though I had the doors shut between the sunroom and my dining room, trying to keep the dust and noise at a minimum, the fine mist from the sanding seeped in. I felt like Satan was trying really hard to interfere with my Bible reading, singing, and praising God. I totally ignored it and continued to write the words and music as a reminder of the way I should live. I felt inspired by God and titled it "Did Someone See." I pray every day that someone will see God's love in me. That was a time in my life when I stopped regretting what might have been and started really believing God had a plan for my life and that if I trusted in Him, I would find joy along the way.

Joy is an important characteristic of a healthy, godly life. God's word calls us to live a joy-filled life. God's word tells us it is possible to have joy even when experiencing the pain of recovery. During the first three months after Bobby's death, God made it possible for me to experience joy and grief at the same time. My daughter Stefanie was scheduled to go back to work after her daughter, Ava, was born. I had planned to be home from vacation and start keeping Ava on May 20, 2008 (which is the day Bobby died). Needless to say, I didn't make it from Virginia Beach, Virginia, to Nashville, Tennessee, that day. Less than a month later, God made it possible for me to get up early and make the hour-and-a-half drive to keep my precious grandbaby. I took my cards and paperwork with me and worked on them while Ava was asleep. I told her stories about Pa Harden. One day after we got home from our neighborhood stroll, I sat her in her carrier on the deck and read to her from one of my grief books. When I read something that made me cry, Ava would start laughing. The louder I read, the louder she laughed, and pretty soon I was laughing too. I think of this so many times when I feel sad about something, and it always makes me smile and warms my heart.

There is one essential requirement for living a joy-filled life—obedience. When I started seeking God's will for my life and taking His commandments seriously, joy started creeping back into my life.

Deuteronomy is one of my favorite books in the Bible because it is a handbook for rebuilders. Many times our future is based on what we learned from the past and how we live in the present. It is a book about hope; it's all about making a fresh start. I can so associate my life with the Israelites who had been wandering around in the wilderness for forty years to accomplish an eleven-day journey. In every life there are moments when it is essential to move on. In rebuilding a life, we must be careful to advance according to God's schedule. It's exciting to be able to start over again knowing that God's grace in the process is unlimited. The Israelites must have been ecstatic when God brought them to the edge of the Promised Land. They were given another chance to begin again. They must have been so thankful for Moses, their wise, godly leader who encouraged them to use their past experiences to set their faith on fire. I thank God for the godly leaders and pastors who encouraged me. He directed the people and gave them detailed instructions on how to move forward and look to the future. He also reminded them to be careful and give God the glory when life gets better. That's exactly what I'm trying to do by writing this book. Deuteronomy 31:8 (NLT) is a scripture I memorized and quoted often when I was going through the muddy seasons in my life: "Do not be afraid or discouraged for the Lord will personally go ahead of you. He will be with you, he will neither fail you nor abandon you." He was speaking to Joshua who became Israel's leader.

There was a time in my life when I concluded that joy was not going to happen to me. When I starting looking up scriptures about joy, I realized God promises us joy. It is God's purpose for our life. It happens when we trust God's plan for our life. Psalm 126:5 (NLT) says, "Those who plant in tears will harvest with shouts of joy." Lewis Smedes says, "Only the heart that hurts has a right to joy." Those two quotes in the front of the book I picked up to prepare to lead my small group hit me like a ton of bricks as I was having second thoughts about leading the class. I always get nervous and worry about saying the wrong thing. I prayed about it and asked God to fill me with the Holy Spirit to get me through the class.

When we all left after the closing prayer singing "Down in My Heart," I knew I'd done okay. I wrote down the definition of joy that was shared in our study by the author and placed it over my sun visor as a reminder of these powerful truths about joy. I read, "Joy is the settled assurance that God is in control of all the details of my life, the quiet confidence that ultimately everything is going to be all right, and the determined choice to praise God in all things."

I left the parking lot thanking God for His guidance in helping me lead the group. My heart was full of joy as I began thanking Him for mending my broken heart and making something beautiful of my life.

I met with my care receiver that same afternoon and shared with her about joy as she had some good news and some bad to share about her situation at that time. It was a perfect example of how sorrow and joy can both be experienced at the same time. As she talked and I listened, I could see how much she has grown in her faith over the past year. She is learning to the lean on Jesus just like I did years ago. I could see God molding her into the person she will become someday. I could see her becoming a Stephen minister someday and helping others. I could see God healing her and helping her to make wise decisions that will impact not only her personal life but the world. I can see God taking her brokenness and making something beautiful of her life.

When I was a young believer, I thought I had to go to some foreign country to do mission work for God. I so admire those who do, but God is using me where He needs me most. He knew geography was not my best subject. He knew I could better serve Him through my church, which is only five minutes from my house. He has taken my messy life and is using me to bring joy into someone's life right in my backyard. I think that's pretty amazing. When I got home after meeting with my care receiver, I sat down at my piano and sang loudly as I played all the verses from "Down in My Heart," laughing as I sang the last verse that my granddaughter Ava likes to sing. "If the devil doesn't like it, he can sit on a tack, sit on a tack, sit on a tack to stay." I remember taking both my granddaughters with me to the nursing home one Tuesday. This was the song my five-year-old granddaughter, Ava, selected for everyone to sing. My oldest granddaughter, Ann-Riley, kept asking me if we could leave. The residents loved it and clapped and applauded when we finished. That's how I keep joy in my heart. To have joy, you must give joy to others. The same goes for money. You must give it away first.

It has taken me a long time to get enough courage to share my personal story. Courage comes from God, who gives it freely to those who are willing to step out in faith in order to help others. I believe joy is a choice, and I choose joy. Giving is also a choice, and I choose giving. The more I give of my time, talent, and money to God, the more blessings He bestows on me. God promises in Luke 6:38a (NIV), "Give and it will be given you." I have the love of Jesus down in my heart to stay! All the money in the world cannot buy joy and peace and contentment. These are gifts from God. Money was created by mankind, and it serves a purpose in society, but like all other earthly things, it should not be coveted. Only God is worthy of worship. Only God can provide true happiness, joy, and peace, and with these three, we can find contentment when we have a right relationship with our Creator.

11

Finding My Purpose

WHO AM I called to be? It's a question I have asked God for years, especially in the retirement season of my life. *Perhaps it is just to love my neighbor as I love myself,* I think this morning as the phone rings and my caller ID tells me it is a friend from Mount Juliet, Tennessee, whose wife had recently passed away. He watched her die with cancer and is having a hard time coping with her death. I was unable to attend the funeral and told him my gift in memory of Jane was that he could call or come visit me anytime. I sent him grief books, cards, and my phone number, calling it his crisis hotline. I invited Doug to come spend the weekend with Tom and me and go to church with us. He took us up on the offer. Doug visited the Sunday Pastor Rick was finishing a sermon series on Pieces (When Broken Becomes Beautiful). The congregation was given a broken tile at the beginning of the service, and we were asked to write something on the back of it and place it on the altar at the end of the service. Doug was so touched by the sermon and service that he asked me to lay his broken piece of tile on the altar for him. He told me later he felt God's presence and healing touch that day and was so thankful he came. I continued to stay in touch, sending him cards and calling him during the holidays and first-year anniversaries.

Doug called this morning, and I gave him an hour of my time. I even took the time to play his favorite hymn, "Leaning on the Everlasting Arms," on the piano for him. Every time he calls, he asks me if I've played the piano lately. This particular morning Doug asked me questions about things I couldn't answer. I mostly shared with him how I made it through all those first anniversaries when my husband and his friend Bobby had died.

When he asked me what I thought heaven was like, I quoted scriptures and read him excerpts from a book I had in the grief section of my mini library. I invited him to come spend the weekend again on the first-year anniversary of his wife's birthday. Doug was raised and worships in a denomination that is different from ours. They do not believe that organ or piano music should be a part of the worship service. He's beginning to come around as this will be his third visit with us to the traditional 11:00 a.m. service, where we sing some of the old hymns he loves so much.

I also shared with Doug how on the first anniversary of Bobby's death, I bought the perfect Hallmark card, wrote a note to Bobby, took it to the cemetery, attached it to a helium balloon, and watched it soar upward toward heaven. My friend loved that idea! I shared how I remembered praying as it lifted up toward the beautiful blue skies that God would let him know how much I loved him and missed him and that I was going to be okay. I sat down on the bench at the foot of the headstone that has Philippians 4:6 (NLT), "Don't worry about anything. Instead pray about everything. Tell God your need and thank Him for all He has done"—lovingly inscribed on it. It was a beautiful day in May, and there was just enough wind to send it up. I watched it until I could see it no more, thinking how short life was and that I needed to make the most of it and enjoy every moment God gave me. I read the inscription I had chosen to put beneath our joint names, "Wherever You Go There You are," reflecting on how Pastor Rick had asked each one of us to all together repeat that phrase at the end of Bobby's funeral service. The saying was one that Bobby spoke often, especially when friends or family would leave after a visit.

I continued to share with Doug over the phone about how I felt God telling me to enjoy the moment. I felt God telling me I was created in love to give love and receive love, yet I was feeling alone and unloved by my distracting thoughts. I had been so focused on feeling sorry for myself that I couldn't see or experience the love God was directing toward me. It was very comforting and healing as I began to focus on how blessed I was to have such a loving family and friends that cared deeply. I felt God's presence in my life sitting there on that bench that day, and I began to understand what being present in the moment really meant. I glanced over at the emblem I had placed on my stone from the Stephen Ministry.

When I was picking out our headstone, the salesman told me I needed to have something inscribed on my side of the stone, especially since Bobby had the National Guard emblem on his. When I told him I couldn't think of anything significant, he suggested a rose and showed me several pictures from a catalog. I laughed and said, "I don't think I want a rose since my life has certainly not been a bed of roses." That day I saw God's love through Jeff, who was so patient and kind and encouraged me not to be in a hurry and think about it. Jeff was a friend of the family and gave up his commission on the sale of the monument. He encouraged me and shared how people often make poor choices when they are grieving and want to hurry and get it over with. I took the catalog home and prayed about it. One day God told me to use the Stephen Ministry logo. I had no idea if it could be duplicated, but there was no problem. I called the Stephen Ministry office in St. Louis, Missouri. The office secretary informed me that she had never been asked that question before and would check with the owner and get back to me. She called me back the same day saying it would be fine. Dr. Haugk even asked if I could send him a picture of it, which I did. He is a pastor and clinical psychologist and the founder of the Stephen Ministry. Dr. Haugk's ministry took on deeper significance as he dealt with the death of his wife in early 2002 after a three-and-a-half-year war with ovarian cancer. He has devoted his professional life to helping congregations train their members to help those who are grieving or struggling with other life difficulties. I was already a trained Stephen minister through my church and became a trained leader later. I knew that was what I wanted on my headstone as I had promised God I would be the best Stephen minister I could be and minister to others who were grieving or struggling with other life difficulties until my dying day. The logo's most dominate feature is the cross of Jesus. It reminds us that Christ is the center of the Stephen Ministry and all Stephen Ministry relationships. The broken person behind the cross symbolizes how we are all broken people, broken by our own sin and imperfections. The Stephen Series logo tells the story of a care receiver's journey from brokenness to wholeness through the transforming power of the cross of Jesus. It is a simple reminder that it is not the Stephen minister who restores a person to wholeness. Rather, it is only through the cross of Jesus that a person can be made whole. The whole person in front of the cross signifies the wholeness we encounter through the transforming power of the cross of Jesus. It is only through Jesus and his life, death on the cross, and resurrection that we who are broken people are made whole. The circle is a symbol of God's eternal and never-ending love for us. God's love surrounds us, holds us, and heals us, with the cross of Jesus at the center of that love. For it was Jesus, God's Son, who allowed himself to be broken on the cross to save us from our sin and give us the opportunity to be restored to wholeness through Him.

That logo has been my inspiration these past few years. It gave me courage then, and it gives me courage today. It gives me hope and strength to help others.

I realized when I hung up the phone today that I was fulfilling my purpose and serving God diligently. I was going the extra mile to show His love to others, especially those who were grieving. I was becoming more like Jesus, and that made me feel wonderful.

Courage is not something we are born with. It is something we earn when we go through tough times and discover they weren't so tough after all. It makes you brave enough to do things you would never have done on your own. It is a promise from God's holy word. Joshua 1:9 is a scripture I have framed and read often. "Be strong and courageous, do not be frightened or dismayed, for the Lord your God is with you wherever you go."

I attended the Connect to Serve Ministry Fair at my church with a joyful attitude. No one signed up to serve at my Stephen Ministry table. I came home and shared my disappointment with Tom, whom I had left home alone with the piano tuner. The piano tuner had been in the process of tuning my piano when it was time for me to leave for the ministry fair, so Tom stayed home with him as he finished the tuning. I sat down to play a tune on my piano to see if I could tell a difference in how it sounded now. I randomly picked out a song called "Our Best" and attempted to play it just like the instructions at the top of music, which said, "With dignity." I sang as I played.

> Hear ye the Master call, Give me thy best… For be it great or small, that is the test. Do then the best you can… Not for reward… Not for the praise of man… But for the Lord. Every work for Jesus will be blest… But he asks from everyone his best. Our talents may be few…These may be small…But until Him is due… Our best, our all.

I knew I had done my best. God was in control of the Stephen Ministry, and He would provide the right people at the right time to grow our ministry. Just like I have to pay a price to have my piano tuned, I have to pay a price to keep my heart in tune with God every day to find God's purpose for my life. By serving Him daily, He rewards me with joy and contentment in my life. One year later there were seven people who signed up for the Stephen Ministry class to start in the fall.

It's not an easy road we are traveling, but we are the ones who make it hard. When I learned to trust God and let Him guide my thoughts and actions and rely on His strength and will for my life, I found the real meaning of joy. Stress has always been a normal part of my life. In 2 Corinthians 12:9, it tells me that His strength is made perfect in our weakness.

God has done a lot of work on me over the years to help me control my stress, being the codependent person that I am. I look to Him every day for help. I find myself repeating over and over again, "I can do all things through Christ who strengthens me." I try to ignore those who discourage me and say negative things about me. I look for ways God is protecting me every day, which helps me keep Him first place in my life. He gives me strength to make it through life's adversities. I'm on a journey with Christ and trust Him to see me through whatever comes my way. I always pray before I make any important decisions, knowing my life might have been different if I had done that in the past. I can't change my past, but I can change my future. I read this quote somewhere: "If you don't leave your past in the past, it will destroy your future. Live for what today has to offer, not for what yesterday has taken away." I've learned to leave the past in the past. I've been forgiven, and I've forgiven those who have hurt me, but most importantly I've forgiven me.

Prayer is a must. There is no other way to power but by prayer. I have seen in my personal life how prayer moves God and how God moves people. I had to first understand the importance of prayer and how to pray. The fifth chapter of James tells me prayer is one of the most powerful tools God has given us. Prayer is essential in the process of putting our broken life back together. The apostle James tells us if we are happy, we should sing praises. He tells us if we are sick, we should call the elders of the church to pray over us, anointing us with oil in the name of the Lord, and the Lord will make you well. And if you have committed sins, you will be forgiven. Healing comes when we admit our sins to God and look to Him for help. We must also pray with confidence. The book of Daniel 1:6–20 tells us how Shadrach, Meshach, and Abednego saw the power of God when they were thrown into a blazing furnace by Nebuchadnezzar, one of the greatest conquerors in the history of the world, when they wouldn't bow down to a statue. We must also model a life of prayer, so others will follow. "As a man prays, so is he" by A. W. Tozer says it best. Money can never buy what I need, nor what I want. It warmed my heart when a member of small group asked me personally to pray privately for a specific need. She told me she knew what a prayer warrior I was and felt comfortable asking me. Perhaps it was because I had shared with my small group over the years the many ways God had answered my prayers. I pray believing that God will answer in a way that is best for me and everyone else involved.

Taking my eyes off myself, stepping out of my comfort zone, and serving those who could not necessarily give back was a vital part of my healing process. I would find the answers to what God wanted me to do with the rest of my life, the prayer I had prayed so diligently. The fact that the events of my life had broken me and I had suffered gave me the answer to my prayer. I began to see myself as someone God could use to make this crazy, mixed-up, broken world a little bit better. As I continued to serve God by playing the piano at the nursing home, I began to feel like I had a purpose and that my life really mattered. By becoming involved in my ministries, small groups, and volunteer programs at church, I began to see God's purpose for my life. Retirement had given me the perfect opportunity to spend more time with my family and grandchildren, and I feel blessed. By serving others, I was reminded that life was not about me. I would discover my true identity by emptying my life into the lives of others who were less fortunate than me. I was learning to become a little more like Jesus. As I learned to depend on God, I began to see His fingerprints on my life. I began to see how He was working behind the scenes to put the pieces of my life back together, as only He can do. When I meet with my new care receiver each week, I see God's healing grace flowing through me. She told me at our last meeting I was an answered prayer and that she was certain God sent me to her. That made me feel pretty special. We always pray and read scripture together, and today we read from 2 Corinthians 9. God spoke to me in verse 8 (NIV): "And God is able to make all grace abound to you, so that in all things at all times, having all that you need, you will abound in every good work."

God spoke to me through this verse by telling me I would be rewarded for helping someone else. He tells us the more spiritual seeds we plant by generously helping others, the greater will be our harvest of spiritual fruit. God never forces us to give; he wants us to give with willing hearts. God is not only interested in what we do but also in why we do it. You may be one of those persons whose life may be in ruins, and you think you don't have much to offer people in need. I felt that way, especially when I was grieving and going through financial loss. But even if we have nothing else to give, we can share our story of how God gave us a second chance. As little as this may seem to us, it may be the gift of life to someone who is broken and in need of God's forgiveness and grace.

In May 2013, I was asked to be a prayer coordinator for the women's retreat. The invitation read, "A Time out for Restoration—A weekend with the Shepherd—Centered around the 23rd Psalm." I was given the responsibility of enlisting additional prayer team members, assisting in the commissioning service of team members, organizing team members to pray consistently for requests during the retreat, praying with the leadership team before each teaching session, and being available for prayer throughout the retreat. I would also be asked to assist in the service of healing on Sunday morning. I was overwhelmed, thinking this was way out of my comfort zone. I prayed about it, knowing this was an important leadership role, and finally said yes. I was nervous, especially during the healing service, but God helped me through it. I came home from the retreat feeling refreshed and restored and was glad I said yes. Pastor Sami was our leader in charge. Her sermon was awesome, and I took notes; I felt she was talking especially to me. She shared how we should love ourselves because God made us just the way we are and we have a job to do that no one else can do. She told us to "stop coveting His goodness in someone else and see His goodness in us. When He asks us to do the impossible, He will handle the details. He does His thing with the stuff we got. We can trust God to be more than enough. All we have to do is follow the Good Shepherd. Where He guides, He will provide. He takes care of all the loose ends 'cause he knows our story has the power to touch somebody else." I read those notes again later and was able to turn my insecurities over to God and just be me.

We listened to the testimony of a lady from Nebraska who told her story of how God healed her when she lost her son. I loved how she used the example of how her brain had short-circuited and how God rewired her brain and restored her soul through her love for horses. She shared how God had made it possible through her husband's job transfer from Southern California to Nebraska soon after her son's funeral (a move she did not want to make). She and her husband now run a successful camp for over one hundred kids with autism on their ranch, which is called Still Waters. The ranch already had the name before they bought it. She explained it was God's story, and she just shared with us how she got into it. She ended with "He leads me beside still waters. When I walk through the valley, He restores my soul." The Twenty-Third Psalm has a whole new meaning for me after hearing her powerful testimony. An important part of spiritual growth is to worship and praise God by sharing our personal testimony of how God protected and cared for and guided us through troubled times.

I went to the nursing home on this unusually hot day in June and was so blessed when the first song requested by an elderly lady with an oxygen mask was "The Beautiful Garden of Prayer." I could hear her singing, and when I looked out of the corner of my eye as I played the piano, I saw her raising her hands and eyes upward praising God. I spoke with another wise lady who shared her story with me about how she came to really know Christ and how excited she was about going to heaven. Just as I was leaving, an elderly gentleman came up to me opening his wallet and handing me his last $2. He asked if I would give it to some needy child. I graciously accepted it and promised him I would. I shared a little bit about the Foundry my church was involved with and assured him it would be put to good use. I took the money by the church office afterward and matched it with $2 from my wallet and prayed for Him, as well as the children at the Foundry. I visited the Foundry that afternoon with my tie-group friends from church. I attended the Pastor Parish meeting that night and was honored to be asked to serve on a committee that made such important decisions for our church. Writing this book has made me realize how far I've grown in my faith and how close I've gotten to God. I am happiest when I am serving God!

As I started to grow and mature in my spiritual life, I took it one step and one day at a time. I did have to step out in faith in order to grow. What's in 2 Peter 1:5–7 (NKJV) helps me in my journey—"But also for this reason, giving all diligence, add to your faith virtue, to virtue knowledge, to knowledge self-control, to self-control perseverance, to perseverance godliness, to godliness brotherly kindness, to brotherly kindness love."

Wherever you are in your spiritual life journey, I encourage you to take a step up today. Add something that will make you a little more in the image of Jesus Christ. Since I became a servant, first and last, God has changed me from the inside out. He has taken my scars and turned them into stars for His glory. It takes courage to step up and step out in faith to do the work God calls us to do. It takes nerve to serve, but the reward is great. Looking back over the past six years since Bobby died, I see clearly how God has shaped my life, and I have discovered new depths of meaning and purpose. I just step up, suit up, and show up. I choose to serve God first with a generous spirit and put on the breastplate of righteousness. Jesus tells us we must give to our fellow man with a generous spirit, something for which we can get no pay. Luke 14:12–14 (WBT) states it pretty clearly.

> When you give a lunch or dinner, don't invite only your friends, your family, your other relatives, and your rich neighbors. At another time they will invite you to eat with them, and you will be repaid. Instead, when you give a feast, invite the poor, the crippled, the lame and the blind. Then you will be blessed because they have nothing and cannot pay you back.

God extends His saving grace and blessing to all people, including the poor and the handicapped of society, who in almost every case are ignored, even abused. Extending mercy to these people will be rewarded by God. I thought of this verse this morning on my way to the nursing home. I normally only commit to one hour on Tuesdays, but Reverend Jessie asked me to come on Thursday as he couldn't be there. I've had a busy week and almost said no. I'm glad I said yes because I felt the presence of God in that place as I shared a story with them from the upper room based on Mark 10:15b (NIV): "Anyone who will not receive the Kingdom of God like a little child will never enter it." It was about a four-year-old who came to her mother with a broken toy and asked her to fix it. When the mother explained to her daughter she probably couldn't fix it, the child responded, "Mom, let's pray to Jesus to fix it." The mother told her they could pray, but Jesus probably wouldn't fix it, and she responded, "Let's pray anyway." I understand why Jesus told his disciples that to enter the kingdom of heaven, they must become like a little child. I asked who among those gathered in the activity room had grandchildren. When most of them raised their hands and smiled, I sat down at the piano and played "Jesus Loves the Little Children." I was blessed as they sang loudly, and most of them knew the words by heart. I challenged them all, as well as myself, to remember to pray with the faith of a child. If I hadn't gone that day, I would have missed out on a special blessing from God.

12

Letting Go

I will turn their mourning into gladness, I will give them comfort and joy instead of sorrow.

JEREMIAH 31:13 (NIV) is a verse of scripture I read often. I memorized God's promise to me like this: "I will turn Trudy's mourning into gladness, I will give Trudy comfort and joy instead of sorrow." It became a personal promise to me and gave me hope. Saying that verse and over again really helped me believe it would happen.

Grieving the loss of a loved one, whether it be a divorce or death, is one of the most challenging things I've ever done. Grieving is not easy. Grief really never ends. In time, the intense pain subsides and memories bring more smiles than tears. Eventually God brought joy back into my life. Grief takes time, but you don't compare your grief to someone else's. Grief is a process—not a race. I found sharing my grief with others and with God leads to facing the loss, and talking about it is the way that leads to healing. Talking is healing; grieving people need to talk about their feelings and their loved ones over and over again. Coping with loneliness was the most difficult part for me. That's when I found myself reaching out to my fellow Stephen Ministers and most importantly reaching out to God. This path of openness became my road to peace and understanding.

Not long after Bobby died, I went to my Stephen Ministry meeting broken and in need of a caring Christian friend. One of my fellow Stephen ministers told me that the Bible says God would be my husband when I shared how I felt so alone. She told me it said so in the book of Isaiah and gave me the chapter and verse. God spoke to me that night when I went home and read Isaiah 54:4–6 (NLT).

> Fear not; you will no longer live in shame. Don't be afraid, there is no more disgrace for you. You will no longer remember the shame of your youth and the sorrows of widowhood. For your creator will be your husband, the Lord of Heaven's armies is his name. He is your Redeemer. "For the Lord has called you back from your grief as though you were a young wife abandoned by her husband, so says your Lord, the Holy One of Israel, the God of all the earth."

Under the Old Testament Law, when someone lost freedom, property, or a spouse because of a disaster or a debt, the next of kin was looked to as their redeemer. If the property had been lost because of inability to pay, the redeemer would pay for it and return it to the original owner. If a woman lost her husband, the redeemer would marry her, providing her with protection and love. This is a promise I held on to. Isaiah 54:10 (NLT) is another passage I clung to: "For the mountains may move and the hills disappear, but even then my faithful love for you will remain. My covenant of blessing will never be broken says the Lord, who has mercy on you."

God became my Redeemer, the restorer of my losses. He is Lord of all. When we give God our past, He will make up for all we have lost. He can fill the empty places in our heart. I dwelled on those verses and read them a lot, asking God to take away my loneliness and grief. I had tried coping with the loneliness on my own. I kept busy during the day, but it was the nights that got to me. The silence drove me crazy. I would hear every creak in the house. Every time the bush beneath my bedroom window brushed against the house, I would think it was someone trying to break into my house. I turned on the TV just to fill the silence. One particular night I remember turning off the TV and trying to pray myself to sleep. I always slept in the middle of the bed because I couldn't stand to sleep on Bobby's side or mine. I started out by thanking God for all the good memories and eventually drifted off to sleep. I suddenly woke up seeing Jesus's face and feeling his loving arms around me, telling me He would take care of me. Most people would say that was just a dream, and it very well could have been, but I took it as a sign from God telling me to trust in Him. My life seemed to get better after that.

I have learned from my journaling over the years that it takes much more concentration and focus to write something down than merely trying to remember it. What I didn't realize until I started writing this book is how much good has come from all the bad stuff. Looking back over my journals and scrapbooks now, I can see how God was there for me all the time, even when I didn't realize it. I see His Grace written all over the pages of my journals. Writing over the years has helped me a lot, especially during the painful periods of my life. It was therapeutic, like me being my own psychiatrist and understanding it differently in the process. I see recovery. I see how God has taken the broken pieces of my life and made me into the person I am today. I see healing. He has made it easier for me to empathize with a lot of people I must deal with. Being involved in the Stephen Ministry, I have grown to respect the importance and validity of the unfolding journey of each person I have come in contact with. I don't try to fix them and save them from their pain. I just try to do what I think Jesus would do.

I went to the nursing home this Tuesday morning to play the piano for those precious people who have become like family to me. I softly and prayerfully played this song while they were gathering in: "To be like Jesus, / To be like Jesus, /

All I ask / to be like Him. All through life's journey, from earth to glory, / All I ask / To be like Him." Most of the residents there are already in the sitting area waiting for me, but there are some who tell me they don't come out of their rooms until they hear the piano. Some of them have to wait for a nursing home employee to wheel them to the activity room. Some of them are able to wheel themselves in their wheelchairs or walkers. It makes me feel good to know that giving one hour one day a week of my time and talent can make such a difference. I get my greatest joy when I encourage others. When I see the expressions on their faces as they sing praises to God, I know I am doing what Jesus would want me to do. I am becoming more like Jesus.

Another year has come and gone, and this New Year's Eve I find myself reflecting on the many ways God has answered my prayers. I'm smiling as I write because I see how He answered in the ways that were best for me. It gives me blessed assurance that He is alive and active in my life. It proves that He loves me more than I could ever imagine. I don't make New Year's resolutions anymore. I make Christ-centered commitments instead. This year I made a commitment to God and myself not to let life's problems or other people's problems interfere with my goal to write this book. I have a Secret Gratitude Book, which is a powerful tool I use to transform my life into joy. I use it periodically and write all the things down I am grateful for now. Writing them down helps me feel gratitude deep in my heart. When I have finished the my Gratitude Now list, I move to the opposite page and write down my Gratitude Intentions list for all the things I want to come into my life. I write them in the same way, as though I already have them now. It is impossible to bring more good into your life if you are feeling ungrateful for what you already have. If you have feelings like jealousy, resentment, dissatisfaction, or feelings of not being enough, those negative feelings cannot bring you what you want. If you want a new car, for instance, and you are not grateful for the one you have, more than likely if you do get the new car, it won't give you any more satisfaction than the one you were not so grateful for. That's how it works for me, anyway. Every time I've complained, blamed, and criticized someone else for my negative emotions, it has backfired on me. I can't be grateful without focusing on the one who created me and gave me everything I have on this earth. Using my Gratitude Book is similar to my "something for God to do" box I talked about earlier, except I write down my prayer requests and wait for them to come true. I'm amazed at how God has provided the items in my Gratitude Intentions list, not exactly as I expected but even better. God wants to give us everything we need to live a full life. The more I pray and the more I praise and serve God, the more good He brings into my life.

New Year's Eve just happened to fall on Tuesday this year, and just like Christmas Eve, I found myself looking forward to playing the piano at the nursing home. Years ago I would never have thought of visiting a nursing home on New Year's Eve.

This year I found myself looking forward to going. We sang "Leaning on the Everlasting Arms," and Revered Jessie, who has been coming for over eighteen years to share the gospel with the residents, quoted Deuteronomy 33:27 (KJV), "The Eternal God is thy refuge, and underneath are the everlasting arms: and he shall thrust out the enemy before thee; and shall say, Destroy them." I leaned on God's Everlasting Arms, and now I'm encouraging others to do the same. I thank God for using the dark valleys of my life to strengthen my faith and allowing me to lean on His Everlasting Arms. My favorite comfort scripture is 2 Corinthians 1:3–4 (NIV), "Praise be to… the God of all comfort, who comforts us in all our troubles, so that we can comfort those in any trouble with the comfort we ourselves have received from God." This tells me He comforts us in all our troubles, not just some of our troubles. God knows I've had a few, and He understands and identifies with them all. He has walked where we walk, lived where we live, and faced what we feel. He is worthy of our trust and able to deliver us from any and all our painful circumstances. When I allowed God to shape my life, I discovered new depths of meaning and purpose. I pray that every time I make a mark on life, it will be for God.

Once I started living daily in the light of the cross and the resurrection, my thoughts and attitudes and even the way I responded to troubles and cares changed dramatically. My life has a purpose and sense of direction. Knowing that heaven is my final destination gives me hope and encouragement to persevere through life's hardships and heartaches. Knowing that if I faithfully serve God, love people, and give generously like he asks me to do, I have a secure inheritance waiting for me in heaven. When I was baptized as a child, I couldn't imagine how God was going to keep up with all those names he had to write in the Lamb's book of life, which the preacher talked about. Today I get it. If there is one thing I'm sure about, it is that there is no confusion in heaven. I read in Revelation 2:17b (NIV), "I will also give him a white stone with a new name written on it." That tells me that I will be given a new name when I get to heaven. I was so relieved when I learned that. I've changed my last name so many times that I didn't know if God would let me in. I'm so glad I got that cleared up. When God says he will make all things new, he means it. I will have a new home, a new body, a new life, and yes, a new name. I will look better and feel better than I ever have.

"But we do know that we will be like Him, for we will see Him as He really is" from 1 John 3:2 assures me I will be like Christ in character, and that's all I need to know. I'll become the person God ultimately intended me to be. That very thought motivates me to faithfully serve my Lord, knowing that my time and effort will be rewarded. I pray that if you have gotten this far in reading my book, you will be encouraged, not disheartened. If you truly desire to become more like Christ but your progress is slow like mine, don't give up. If you have given up on God completely, please read

Jude 1:24 (NIV): "God is able to keep you from stumbling and to make you stand in the presence of His glory blameless with great joy." I found this scripture when I was looking for joy scriptures and needing joy back in my life.

As a Christian, I don't worry about the future because 1 Peter 1:3–7 (NLT) tells me all I need to know about my future and hope of eternal life:

> All praise to God, the Father of our Lord Jesus Christ. It is by His Great Mercy that we have been born again, because God raised Jesus Christ from the dead. Now we live with great expectation, and we have a priceless inheritance—an inheritance that is kept in heaven for you, pure and undefiled, beyond the reach of change and decay. And through your faith, God is protecting you by His power until you receive this salvation, which is ready to be revealed on the last day for all to see. So be truly glad. There is a wonderful joy ahead, even though you have to endure many trials for a little while. These trials will show that your faith is genuine.

I pray the words on this page will encourage you to get involved and live your life for Christ if you are not already. Jesus is waiting to live His life through you. Christ allowed me to survive my losses and is giving me an amazing opportunity to serve Him and do what He has called me to do. He can help you too if you ask Him to. He's only a prayer away. The following song is very special to me because I've played it on my piano and sang it so many times. It gave me inspiration and hope during my darkest hours. I'm praying it might help you too.

I Asked the Lord

I asked the Lord to comfort me when things weren't going my way. He said to me, I will comfort you and lift your cares away. I asked the Lord to walk with me when darkness was all that I knew. He said to me, never be afraid, for I will see you through. I didn't ask for riches, He gave me wealth untold / The moon, the stars, the sun, the sky; and gave me eyes to behold. I thank the Lord for everything, and I count my blessings each day; He came to me when I needed Him / I only had to pray: And He'll come to you, if you ask Him to / He's only a prayer away!

13

Using the Secret Power

My life has been a bittersweet mix of love, sadness, fear, wonderment, hope, and joy. Writing this book has been one of the most difficult things I've ever done. It has forced me to relive my painful past, but it has also strengthened my faith. I'm amazed at how far I've come over the years and how God is using my broken life to help others.

There was a period in my life when my faith was weak, especially after my divorce when I was bitter and angry. I wrestled a great deal with guilt and blamed myself for my failed marriage. I stopped going to church because it was so painful for me to sit in a church pew with my girls and have people wonder where my husband was. I was raised in a church that didn't believe in marrying again after divorce, and

I vowed I would never marry again. I sure got that one wrong. I hadn't started the forgiveness process yet. It wasn't until I learned to love myself first that I learned the true meaning of grace and just how much God really does love us.

When I went through the short courtship and marriage and death of my second husband, I learned the true meaning of real love, the kind of love that God teaches us about in the thirteenth chapter of Corinthians.

Several years ago, a dear friend and member of my small group gave me a copy of 1 Corinthians 13:4–7, except where the word *love* is written, she inserted my name instead. I have it framed and hanging on the wall in my dining room, where I can read it every day. It's all about love! It reminds me not of who I am but of the person I want to become. I want to be more like Jesus.

> Trudy is patient. Trudy is kind. Trudy does not envy. Trudy does not boast. Trudy is not proud. Trudy is not rude. Trudy is not self-seeking. Trudy is not easily angered. Trudy keeps no records of wrongs. Trudy does not delight in evil, but rejoices with the truth. Trudy always protects. Always trusts. Always hopes. Always Perseveres.

Love never fails. Chapter 13 defines real love, and the fourteenth chapter of 1 Corinthians shows how love works. My Bible tells me that love is more important than all the spiritual gifts exercised in the church. Great faith, acts of dedication or sacrifice, and miracle-working power produce very little without love.

Our society confuses love and lust. Paul explains in the thirteenth chapter of his first letter to the church at Corinth that love is more than a feeling, it is choosing to behave in loving ways. It is a fruit of the Holy Spirit produced in our life as we yield to God. No one loves perfectly, but we must learn how to love others and stop waiting for them to love us. When we choose to act in loving ways, the emotions will follow, and we will discover that our love will be returned.

Perhaps you are reading this final chapter today and have given up on love. You may have waited to find love, only to be disappointed. Maybe your loved ones have hurt you so badly you are still numb from the pain. Once you understand just how much God loves you and turn your pain over to Him, you will find yourself able to reach out to love again. God will help you find ways to deal with your past issues. He can even use our past failures and brokenness to teach us something for His glory.

Growing up, Jackie Kennedy was my hero. I have read almost all her books, as well as the stories and articles that were written about her life. I carried a quote of hers in my wallet for years that read, "You should marry the first time for love, the second time for money, and the third time for companionship." Now in my mature years, I disagree with her statement. I say you should never marry unless it is for love. I married four times for love. I have loved all my husbands in different ways and different seasons of my life. They are all unique in their own way. Isn't that ironic? God created all of us in His own image, yet He made each of us uniquely different. Sometimes it is hard to love those we love, but God's love is always the same. He helps us love people, even our husbands, when they are unlovable. My journey through life has taught me what Jackie meant when she said, "I think my biggest achievement is that, after going through a rather difficult time, I consider myself comparatively sane." My favorite quote from Jackie is, "If you bungle raising your children, I don't think whatever else you do well matters very much."

My sister Barbara called me four years after my third husband, Bobby, died and asked if I would speak at a mother-daughter banquet at the little country church where she and I grew up. My first inclination was to say no, remembering how nervous I was when I gave my testimony at a Celebrate Recovery meeting in front of approximately one hundred people. She told me they were expecting around one hundred to attend. I prayed about it and stepped out of my comfort zone once again and said yes. I fretted over what to talk about, but since it was a mother-daughter banquet, I immediately thought of my mother and 1 Corinthians 13:13 (NIV): "These three things remain, faith, hope, and love, but the greatest of these is love."

I chose to talk about a mother's love. I practiced my speech in front of the mirror before I left the house and in the car during the hour-and-a-half ride to the church on Friday night. I prayed for strength as I pulled into that little country church that held so many memories. I was so nervous during the meal that I could hardly eat. The ladies had prepared a wonderful meal and decorated beautifully with fresh flowers on each table. I remember feeling a little sad as I reflected back on the last Mother's Day banquet I had attended with my mother before she went to be with the Lord. I reminded myself I would be honoring her today, and that made me even more nervous. I was glad when it came time for me to take the podium after the opening song of "If I Could Hear My Mother Pray Again." I wanted to get it over with.

I started by telling them why I chose to talk about a mother's love and began putting on an old-time apron and giving them a history lesson on Grandma's apron.

"I don't think our kids today know what an apron is," I said. I continued to share the following: "The principal use of Grandma's apron was to protect the dress underneath because she had so few, and it was easier to wash aprons than dresses. But along with that, it served as a pot holder for removing hot pans from the oven. It was wonderful for drying children's tears and, on occasion, was even used for cleaning out dirty ears. From the chicken coop, the apron was used for carrying eggs and fussy chicks. And when company came, those aprons were ideal hiding places for shy kids. Those big old aprons wiped many a perspiring brow bent over the hot woodstove. Chips and kindling wood were brought into the kitchen in that apron. From the garden, it carried all sorts of vegetables.

After the peas had been shelled, it carried out hulls. And in the fall, the apron was used to bring in apples that had fallen from the trees. And when the weather was cold, Grandma wrapped it around her arms to keep her warm. And when unexpected company drove up the road, it was surprising how much furniture that old apron could dust in a matter of seconds. When Grandma walked out onto the porch, waved her apron, the menfolk knew it was time to come in from the fields to dinner."

I told them it would be a long time before someone invents something that could replace that old-time apron that served so many purposes. I asked for and got a small show of hands from those who remembered Grandma setting her hot apple pies on the windowsill to cool. I got a good laugh from the group when I said, "Her granddaughters today set their pies on the windowsill to thaw, and they would go crazy trying to figure out how many germs were on that old apron, but I don't think I ever caught anything but love from my grandma's apron."

That broke the ice a little bit for me, and I was able to finish my talk without my voice quivering too much. I was able to talk about my mother, who passed away suddenly in 1991 at the age of seventy-one. I compared her love to the love of Christ. The rest of my talk got easier as I spoke of her love and shared the following with them:

"A mother's love is one of a kind. It begins when her child is born and continues for a lifetime and beyond, which to me is the closest love on earth to that of our heavenly Father. The bond we share with her is the first and, in many ways, the most important relationship we will ever experience with anyone. It's a lot like the love of God, which is far greater than any human can explain. It's indescribable. A mother is the foundation of life and family. We have our beginning in her. Nurtured by her warmth and caring, we thrive and grow knowing that there is someone who loves us unconditionally, knowing there is someone who will always be there for us no matter what. And when trials come our way, who is the first person we call? Our mother, right?

"I remember at first I didn't trust anyone to watch my kids but my mother, and when my kids were born, it was my mother whom I wanted there with me. My kids were born in the era where fathers and grandfathers belonged in the waiting room. When I had surgery and lived several miles away, it my mother whom I wanted there with me. I called, and she came, of course. She rearranged her schedule to come cook, clean, and get my kids off to school, to stay as long as I needed her. And when both my daughters had miscarriages, who do you think they called? Me, of course, and when my two granddaughters were born, both my daughters wanted me to be in the delivery room with them. Two of the happiest moments of my life were when I witnessed each of my granddaughters' births. When my first granddaughter, Ann-Riley, was born, my daughter Stefanie, my son-in-law Mark, and I gathered around Alison's bed when Alison held her newborn baby for the first time. We all held hands and offered up a prayer of thanks and celebration to God for the awesome miracle of birth we had just experienced. One year and eleven months later the scene was repeated when my second granddaughter, Ava, was born. This time my daughter Alison, my son-in-law Lance, and I gathered around Stefanie's bed and once again praised God for the miracle we call Ava. It was just as awesome as when my first granddaughter was born. Both times I couldn't help but reflect back on how different the scene was when my two daughters were born. I was isolated and unconscious when both my daughters were born, and I was the last person in the immediate family to witness the miraculous results of their births."

I shared how in this season of my life, God was the one I called when I had good news or bad because His love was even greater than that of my mother's. "He rejoices with me when the news is good and grieves with me when the new is bad. Just like my mother's love, His love never fails. I believe God shows His best love through mothers and grandmothers. I have a favorite bookmark that says, 'Grandmothers are God's favorite people. He gives them children to love, and grandchildren to love them back.' It's God's way of giving us a second chance to correct all the mistakes we made raising our own kids, which brings me back to the story of Grandma's apron." I took off the old-time grandmother's apron I had borrowed from my sister to help get my point across, and it got stuck in my earring while trying to do so, which made for another good laugh.

I continued to share with the Mother's Day audience a little bit of my personal story and how I thanked God for giving me such a wise and godly mother who was a prayer warrior, a mother who trusted in the Lord with all her heart and did not rely on her own understanding, which was what one of her favorite scriptures from Proverbs 3:5 said, "I have no doubt I am the person I am today because of my mother's prayers. I know she was praying for me when I learned how to play the piano at this same little country church all those years ago. God was preparing me then to learn those old hymns that I play at the nursing home today."

I closed my speech by talking about Mary, the mother of Jesus. I spoke about how Mary must have wondered why God picked her. I think it was because He knew Mary would love Jesus best. The Bible doesn't tell us a lot about Mary, but there are a couple of scriptures that I found interesting, which led me to believe she spent a lot of time praying for her Son. I'm sure she prayed for strength and courage for him to get through his trial and crucifixion. Acts 1:12–13 tells us after Christ was taken up into heaven, the disciples immediately returned to Jerusalem and had a prayer meeting. Verse 14 (NIV) says, "They all joined together constantly in prayer, along with the women and Mary the Mother of Jesus, and with his brothers." Then I spoke of the joy Mary must have felt when her Son ascended into heaven and the peace that she must have felt, a peace that passes all understanding. I compared it to the peace I remember seeing on my mother's face one Memorial Day weekend when I was visiting the cemetery with her. My mom was laying roses she had lovingly cut from her garden on the grave of her firstborn child. I asked my mother how she got through burying her precious baby at thirteen months old. She told me when I had lived as long as she and been through difficult times, I would realize there were a lot of things worse than death. I remember my mother looking up and pointing toward heaven as she said, "I know where she is, and I know I'll see her again someday." I thank God every day for my Christian heritage. That is the most important legacy we can pass on to our children and grandchildren. They can see God's love through us, and our love will go with them forever and ever.

I was so relieved when the service was over. Just before I left, the ladies of the church presented me with a check which more than covered my expenses. They also gave me a new large-print edition of The Daily Bible. I couldn't believe it when I read "In Chronological Order 365 Daily Readings" on the front cover. I shared with them how I had been wanting one of those Bibles ever since a friend at church shared hers with me at a Bible study class. I started reading it the very next day and read the entire Bible in one year.

Driving home that Friday night, I thanked God for getting me through the talk and for blessing me so with my new Bible. It's amazing how God blesses us with what we need when we need it, especially when we step out in faith and obey Him.

Love and loss go hand in hand. Times of sorrow and grief are felt in every life, but God has made provisions for each of us in our loss. Not only does He place His shoulder next to ours beneath the heavy load of tears and heartbreak, He brings us comfort and solace of friends and family. With time, joy lessens sorrow, and life overtakes death. We realize our hearts will live to sing again. That too is God's promise, that even in our darkest hour, a brighter dawn will soon be breaking. Psalm 27:13–14a (NKJV) tells me to be patient and wait on the Lord. "I would have lost heart, unless I had believed that I would see the goodness of the Lord in the land of the living. Wait on the Lord; Be of good courage, and He shall strengthen your heart."

I can understand what Paul was talking about in 2 Corinthians 7:11a (MSG) when he writes, "And now, isn't it wonderful all the ways in which this distress has goaded you closer to God?" It was through the really difficult times in my life that I saw God for who He truly is. When my faith was tested, I was forced to look up at the One who could see me through. During my times of heartache and brokenness, I saw the value I had in God's eyes. I got a glimpse of just how much God really does love me. Looking back over my scrapbook of life, I see God as my Ultimate Provider, especially when money was tight. I see God's love today in the many ways He continues to bless me.

The decision to move on and find a new partner after the death of a beloved spouse is very difficult. Some people choose to remain single. I believe there's no right or wrong decision. That's between you and God. When you are grieving, you don't exactly feel charming and adventurous enough to date. Friends and family sometimes have no problem letting you know whether you are dating too soon or not soon enough. If there are children or grown children or stepchildren involved, you will find yourself wanting to protect them, like I did. Then there comes the guilt of the fact that you still love the one who has died.

I Googled and did a little research on my own and found people who remarry after the death of a spouse report less depression and a greater sense of well-being and life satisfaction. I read a lot of stories from the Bible about widowed women. My favorite story is the love story from the book of Ruth. In the time of the judges, Naomi and her family moved to neighboring Moab to escape a severe famine in Israel. Naomi's husband died there, and her sons married Moabite women. In time, both of her sons also died, leaving Naomi destitute and alone, far from her relatives in Israel. One daughter-in-law, Orpah, returned to her own family; the other one, Ruth, stayed with Naomi to comfort her in her grief.

Grief is hard work; it is painful. People who are grieving need others to grieve with them and comfort them. Ruth's faithfulness to her mother-in-law during this time is indeed striking. She gave up the security of her family in Moab to move and face a future of probable loneliness and poverty in a foreign land, but Ruth's faithfulness yielded the fruits of God's blessing, and Naomi experienced God's comfort and love through her.

Together Ruth and Naomi trusted God to help them, and God came through in His own time. The circumstances through which their desperate needs were met reveal God's unseen hand at work. God led Naomi and Ruth back to Israel, where Ruth met Boaz, her future husband. Not only did Ruth find security and love, but the sadness of Naomi's heart was replaced with joy.

We have all experienced some kind of loss. There are times when we might feel as if the future is hopeless, even after we have given it over to God. As we grieve, we sometimes feel abandoned and bitter toward God and the people around us, even though we know He is working on our behalf behind the scenes.

Our values and needs are different as time goes on, especially after the loss of a spouse. I've learned you don't have to let go of positive feelings about your spouse and previous marriage. Tom and I talk about our previous spouses and share stories, which I find to be comforting and helpful and healing.

Several of my friends have had luck finding a new husband online. When Tom came into my life, I prayed a lot about our relationship. He was a cancer survivor, and I knew my kids were worried about me going through another loss. I'll have to admit, I had mixed feelings at first about taking care of another dying man. I knew he had two adopted kids who were in college, and I didn't know if I had the energy to take on another blended family. The worry list went on and on. I finally gave it up to God and took another chance on love. Three years later, as I am finishing my book, I can truly say I'm glad I said yes to God and yes to Tom when we vowed to keep God in first place and center of our lives.

I feel blessed to have been loved by four husbands. When I asked Tom why he was attracted to me when we first met, he replied, "It was because of your spirit and mind, but also because you had a suntan, therefore I thought, 'She must like the outdoors.'" He loves to play golf and has even gotten me on the golf course with him.

As I reach the end of my memoir, I'd like to paraphrase the inscription found on Bobby's tombstone. Remember, wherever you are in your life is where you are. I pray that you have already found God's grace and accepted His forgiveness. If not, I urge you to find the fullness of living life for His purpose so that you can glorify Him in all that you do. He is your Creator, Friend, and Savior. I promise you if you make Him number 1 in your life, you will have no regrets. Accept His grace, love Him, read more about Him, pray to Him, trust

Him, and glorify Him. Learn to love, forgive, and understand that true happiness can come from your pain. Live your life the way God so perfectly intended for you to live. He will put the broken pieces of your life back together and make something beautiful.

Acknowledgments

To MY LOVING family.

Tom, I'll always be grateful to God for the snowstorms that kept you off the golf course long enough to help me and inspire me to finish my book. Thank you for loving me, believing in me, and helping me stay grounded in my faith.

To my awesome kids: Stefanie (and husband, Lance), Alison (and husband, Mark). Thank you for hanging in there with me and giving me support. You were forced to navigate rough waters early in your lives. You suffered things no mother ever wants their children to suffer. But seeing my prayers answered for you today gives me great comfort. I am so proud of the wonderful way you parent my precious granddaughters who bring so much joy into my life.

Ava and Ann-Riley, I am so proud of the way you show your love for Jesus at such an early age.

To my parents, Presley and Pauline Chelf, I will always be grateful for your godly example and for teaching me about the love of Jesus.

To my sisters, Barbara and Maurita. Where would I be without you? We've weathered a lot of storms together, and I love you more today than I did yesterday.

To my niece, Amy, who is like a daughter to me and a sister to Stefanie and Alison. There's a special bond that will last forever.

To my nephews—David, Todd, and Weldon—who praised me when I didn't feel praiseworthy.

To my great-nephews—JT, Mason, Clayton, and Talvin and great-niece, Bethany. You are so special to me.

To my blended families. I am so grateful to God for my stepchildren.

Robin, thank you for being there for me when your dad died and for continuing to stay in touch. Bob Jr. (and wife, Pam), thank you for all the memories I hold in my heart. Thank you for sharing Brooke, Sarah, and Ethan with me and allowing me to be their Grana. Thank you for allowing me to be part of your lives and staying in touch.

To my sister-in-law, Judy, who was there to grieve with me and help me when I needed her most.

To my stepdaughter, Jeannie, I would like to say your dad would be proud of you. Even though our time together was short-lived, I will always love you.

To my newest stepchildren, Brant and Holly, thank you for accepting me, loving me, and challenging me once again to live into my faith by opening my heart and my home to you. I love you both.

To my incredible church families and friends. Thank you, Knifley Christian Church, Columbia Christian Church, and Broadway United Methodist Church. Thank you for just being you!

My pastors, staff, music team, Stephen ministers, prayer team, small groups, disciple Bible class, tie group, and God friends. You've prayed for me, laughed with me, but most importantly, you've loved me unconditionally throughout my faith journey.

To my forever friends. You know who you are! Thank you for being there for me in my darkest hours and for being there to celebrate with me during the brightest of times! Only God could have placed you in my life at just the right time—to help put the broken pieces back together.

Thanks to my ex-husband for all the good parts of our life together and for giving me the beautiful daughters and granddaughters that we share today.

Special thanks to Deborah Bard for her mosaic work of art she designed and allowed me to use on the cover of this book. To Meghan Johnston for her photography expertise. To Linda Stauffer for her commitment to the success of my memoir.

Last but certainly not least, this is in memory of my husbands, Jerry and Bobby, who are such an integral part of my story.

Made in the USA
Columbia, SC
17 April 2024

34255533R00098